ZEN AND THE ART OF QUILTING

Exploring Memory and Meaning in Patchwork

by Sandra Detrixhe
Author of *The Everything® Quilting Book*

Adams Media
Avon, Massachusetts

Published by
Adams Media, an F+W Publications Company
57 Littlefield Street, Avon, MA 02322 U.S.A.
www.adamsmedia.com

ISBN: 1-59337-093-8

Printed in Canada.

J I H G F E D C B A

Library of Congress Cataloging-in-Publication-Data
Detrixhe, Sandra.
Zen and the art of quilting / Sandra Detrixhe.
p.   cm.
ISBN 1-59337-093-8
1. Quilting—United States—Miscellanea. 2. Patchwork—United States--Miscellanea.
3. Zen Buddhism. I. Title.
TT835.D477 2004
746.46—dc22
2004005959

This publication is designed to provide accurate and authoritative information with regard to the subject matter covered. It is sold with the understanding that the publisher is not engaged in rendering legal, accounting, or other professional advice. If legal advice or other expert assistance is required, the services of a competent professional person should be sought.

—From a *Declaration of Principles* jointly adopted
by a Committee of the American Bar Association
and a Committee of Publishers and Associations

Many of the designations used by manufacturers and sellers to distinguish their products are claimed as trademarks. Where those designations appear in this book and Adams Media was aware of a trademark claim, the designations have been printed with initial capital letters.

Interior illustrations by Argosy.

This book is available at quantity discounts for bulk purchases.
For information, call 1-800-872-5627.

For my friend Mary Peeler,
who predicted this.

Contents

Acknowledgments

I want to thank all the quilters and others who let me use their stories. I have tried to stay true to what each told me and apologize for any inaccuracies I may have inadvertently made. A special thank you goes to my husband, Joe, for support and suggestions, and for alerting me to several leads. Also thank you to my daughter, Eden, for all her encouragement and creative input as well as for sharing her own quilting stories and unique perspective on the craft. Last, I need to thank my boss, Irene Brown, for encouragement and for letting me take some mornings off to write. I couldn't have done this without all of you.

Introduction

Zen is the Japanese translation of a Sanskrit word meaning "meditation." Zen proposes that we better understand ourselves and hence our place in the world by looking inward, knowing our true selves, and losing ourselves at the same time.

Zen is not a religion, although it is usually associated with Buddhism. It is actually a route toward enlightenment, the aim of Buddhism. But then, Buddhism isn't really a religion, either. You can be a Christian, Jew, agnostic, or anything else and a Buddhist at the same time. In fact, Buddhists believe we are all Buddhists; most of us simply haven't discovered our Buddhist nature, that's all.

Zen is about our innermost life, about reality, about achieving our greatest potential. In Western culture's parlance, we call something Zen if it emphasizes the process over the product because self-discovery awaits in the doing. We call something Zen if it locates connections between seemingly unconnected things or finds dual truths in apparent contradictions because with Zen all things are connected. And we call something Zen if it recognizes the spiritual nature of ordinary acts or activities.

The word *quilt* comes from an Old French word meaning "mattress." Though quilting, or sewing layers of fabric together, originally came from Asia and was influenced by Europeans, our usual image of a quilt as the pieced or patched handmade blanket is very American.

These two seemingly unrelated images, Zen and quilts, come together in meditation mats and sweet dreams under warm quilts. Yet everything about the process of making a quilt, preserving Grandmother's quilt, or giving a quilt to a newborn child can be full of spiritual meaning. Symbolism abounds in the marriage of beauty and function, the joy of a vision fulfilled (though not always as expected), or the union of, say, 612 individual pieces in one quilt.

Making a quilt comes down to the here and now, the moment-to-moment handling of the cloth, the threading of the needle, and the rocking of it back and forth in and out of the cloth. This is at once an activity both absorbing and mind-freeing. This is what meditation is, essentially: quiet surroundings, sitting still, repetitive mental patterns.

Not every quilt is going to be a Zen Quilt. Certainly all of mine aren't. You can't look at my quilts and tell which ones are and which ones aren't. So what do I mean by a Zen Quilt? A Zen Quilt is one begun out of a desire to make it rather than to have it. It is a quilt made with an anticipation of the surprises, rather than a desire to make it just so. In other words, I've let the spirit move me rather than the rules.

If you've never made a quilt before, be assured that it isn't an exact science, and you can do pretty much whatever you want. If you approach it with a spirit of adventure, it'll be a rewarding experience. You don't need to make a big investment. You don't need a sewing machine, although it can speed things along, and you don't need a huge quilt frame, although some kind of hoop is going to make the stitching smoother. You'll need scissors, needles, thread, and faith. Oh, and cloth and batting, but we'll get to all that. Right now, concentrate on the faith part.

If you are an accomplished quilter, consider giving up a little of the perfection your experience has taught you for some recklessness of creativity. What's the quilt you always wanted to do but were afraid would somehow look wrong? What are the color combinations you like that make everyone else cringe? What is the one idea you want to express but haven't figured out how to yet?

Close your eyes, say a prayer, smile, and go for it.

chapter one

Let the
Possibilities Unfold

Fabric Preparation

New fabric requires preparation before you can use it. Machine-wash it. Then to keep it from becoming too wrinkled, cut away the worst of the frayed threads and shake out the fabric before tossing it into the dryer. Pull a thread near one cut edge to find the grain and cut along this line. Fold the fabric in half along the trimmed edge and hold it up to see if the selvages align. If they don't, pull the fabric on the bias until they do. Iron your fabric before cutting out your pieces.

Country Cousins

There's a little fabric store called Country Cousins two half-blocks and catty-cornered across an intersection from where I work. I go there sometimes during my lunch hour, foregoing food in favor of walking among the bolts of fabric or searching through the stacks of remnants and fat quarters.

Quilt making has become my favorite hobby in the past few years. As with any hobby, it's an opportunity to leave my worries behind for an hour, or an afternoon if I'm lucky. The quilt-in-progress will wait for me during the busy times, and I can jump right into it again when things ease up a little.

Quilt making is a whole-brain activity. The left brain is active cutting precise pieces and fitting them together like a puzzle, while the beauty of the quilt and the creativity of sewing appeal to the right brain. I love the feel of the fabric, the look of a well-made seam, and the surprises that sometimes come when fabrics blend in unusual ways. I enjoy counting down the progress: Last week I had 200 pieces to fit together, and now there are only 112. I need something to keep my hands busy while I watch TV, but I also like sitting in a quiet place while I piece or quilt, alone with my thoughts. Antique quilts have always fascinated me, but I appreciate them more now that I've quilted, too.

Psychologists say our hobbies should be, in most respects, the opposite of our work activity. If our work is basically analytical, we need a creative hobby. If our work is physically demanding, we need a restful hobby, and vice versa. The only thing that keeps quilt making from being an ideal hobby for me is the lack of exercise. But at least I walk to the fabric store.

My daughter, Eden, a new convert to quilting, has recently earned a master's degree in political science. Her thesis dealt with women and minorities. For her, quilt making takes on additional meaning. She writes, "A work of art that is also functional, a quilt is in the 'nitty gritty' of everyday life, keeping a child warm, telling a story of a marriage or birth, noting personal memories of dresses worn or flour sacks used. It also tells women's stories at large: Of and for the home, it illustrates the sexual division of labor and gender expectations. Historically, it's one of women's few sanctioned creative outlets and an excuse to get together with other women. The quilting circle or bee was a rare women's forum for whatever topic, perhaps foretelling the feminist consciousness-raising groups of the 1970s. At the same time, a quilt transcends all of that because it is art. Heart and soul, imagination and skill come together to create a work of useable art."

I think for Eden, quilt making is a way of communing with women of another time or honoring them. I can feel that, too, but as I walk the short distance along the midwestern small-town street with the noise of the truck traffic on the highway receding slowly behind me, I have nothing quite so lofty in mind. I want to play.

I often carry small plastic bags that contain swatches from projects that still need one or more fabrics before I can begin. Ever hopeful, I carry the bags with me most of the time in case I have an unexpected opportunity to visit Country Cousins or some other fabric store.

Sometimes I simply walk around the store, seeing what's new or what might jump out at me that I didn't fully notice last time. Bright prints on cool white backgrounds make me think of hot summer days when the roses and zinnias were blooming in my mother's garden. Rusts and browns make me think of standing at the end of our driveway on cool autumn mornings, waiting for the school bus as the fog further muted summer's fading colors.

Sometimes a tiny flowered print will remind me of the sundresses my sister Nora and I wore; hers were always pink or red, and mine were blue. Or a fabric will stir an emotion even though the memory is gone.

The appearance of the fabrics is only part of the pleasure of walking around the store. Different weights of fabrics have different textures, even among the cottons, the traditional fabric for quilting. Some are coated to make them crisp; others are more natural and soft and wrinkly. Still others are so silky I find myself checking the bolt to be sure they are really cotton. But even the coarsest, heaviest cotton is more inviting to the touch than the paper I've spent the morning shuffling.

Strolling among the bolts of fabrics is very comforting after the glare of the computer screen, the harsh demands of the phone, and the routine stress of the office, but only if I enter with the right attitude. I need to be open to the memories and to the comfort, and it takes a conscious decision to do that. One way of describing this decision is to say it's my attempt to live my Zen.

Other quilters I've talked to had similar experiences, though they expressed them differently. Several mentioned liking fabric stores. Teresa LaFlair said she "gets high going to the fabric store." I suspect they are experiencing some of the same escape that I do.

Among other things, Zen is about discovering your greatest potential, your true self—in other words, your Buddhist nature. This discovery is achieved through meditation and living your Zen. At the very foundation of Buddhism are the Four Noble Truths: Life is suffering. Suffering is caused by selfish desires. Selfish desires can be overcome. To overcome them, eight things must be right in your life. Striving to get those eight things right is part of how you go about living your Zen. Those eight things, those keys to happiness, if you will, are perfect subjects for meditation. One of these is alertness.

As I walk the block to the fabric store, I try to leave the office behind in my mind as well as with my body. Unfinished tasks will be remembered when I walk back through the door an hour from now. Pondering them will not make them easier later; in fact, the opposite is often true. I will be able to think them through more quickly after giving my brain a break.

Instead of simply being "not at work," I need to thoroughly be in this place at this time, alert to the possibilities. Without that openness, that alertness, I am simply shopping for a fabric rather than enjoying the store. I am searching for one thing and missing everything else. But with this openness, shopping is a different experience. It sets the imagination free, makes discoveries possible, and, instead of being tiring, it's actually a refreshing experience.

Yin and Yang

Pattern and fabric are the yin and yang of quilt making. They represent equal forces in perfect balance, each one right for the other. Like the chicken and the egg, it doesn't matter which comes first. Either can stimulate your imagination and send you searching for the other.

For me, it's usually the fabric that inspires me. I fall in love with a particular fabric and imagine it as part of a quilt. But that's not always the case. For example, a quilter's catalog advertised the instructions for a pattern called Garden Twist. The fabrics were arranged to look like flowers blooming on a trellis. While it attracted me with its simple beauty, the arrangement itself looked too complicated to try to figure out on my own, so I bought the pattern. Months later I found a morning glory print to use with it.

That is one of my very few pattern-inspired projects, even when I decide, as I often do, that the last thing I need is more fabric and I search for a pattern instead. I really should make this particular decision more often. I've been sewing for years and have accumulated boxes of fabric scraps. I've also inherited three women's scrap collections, giving me scraps from several different eras. So occasionally I'll search for a pattern that will use up some of these scraps, but it's still the fabric (boxes of it!) that makes a particular pattern look intriguing.

The pieced quilt was invented in the first place as a way of getting the most out of every scrap of fabric. Early settlers to North America and later the westward-moving pioneers had no choice. They were far from any source of new fabric unless they wanted to spin and weave it themselves. The first patchwork quilt might have been a quilt whose tears and worn places were patched until the original fabric was nearly hidden.

As civilization with its industry and transportation caught up with the pioneers, whole cloth and two-tone quilts became more the style. Buying new fabric to make a quilt was a sign of prosperity. Multicolored scrap quilts became popular again during the Great Depression, not because of the scarcity of fabric this time, but because of the scarcity of money to pay for it. Still, it's a special joy to make something out of nothing (or almost). I love the notion of following a wonderful old tradition, and I feel, as my daughter describes, a certain bond with resourceful women of the past.

The early quilters passed on traditions through the patterns they invented as well as through the antique quilts themselves. Every quilt pattern has at least one name. Sometimes several slightly different (or occasionally vastly different) patterns will share a name. It's best to think of the names as part of the fun and not be too dogmatic about them. It can seem confusing at first, but just think of it as part of the diverse history of quilting.

The names given to some old patterns make us think of life's journey: Tree of Life, Cross Roads, Way of the World, Guiding Star, Wandering Foot, Friendship Quilt. Of course, there is a reason for this. Women and the occasional man have been expressing their experiences and their feelings through quilts for ages.

Sometimes when I'm searching for a pattern, whether I'm trying to fit it to a fabric or I'm simply looking for a place to start, I visit the craft section of my local library and look through the quilt books there. It's fun to see if any of the names will speak to me in my particular situation. Do I feel like a Windblown Star or more like a Toad in a Puddle? (It's best not to be too serious when you're reading through these names.) If the name doesn't resonate, perhaps the design will.

Generally, however, I have the fabric first and then need to figure out what to do with it. Once, while ostensibly shopping for fabric for a border around a wall hanging quilt I had just finished piecing, I came across an exquisite Victorian-looking print with red roses and cream and gold love letters. Besides the romance of the whole theme of the fabric, I was attracted by the wonderful details in the print. There are blue ribbons and pink bows and little sprigs of lilies-of-the-valley. There were about 5 yards left on the bolt, more than I would need of a single fabric for most quilts, but I went ahead and got it all, imagining the possibilities.

A cynic might call this impulse buying, but a cynic would never make a quilt. You can, after all, buy quilts sewn together in factories for the price of your fabric or less. It has to be a love of the process, the urge of creativity, and a certain amount of optimism that brings you back to the fabric store with a bag of swatches (or two bags or more!) to test your chosen fabrics against whatever attracts you.

Before I could look for fabrics to coordinate with my new Victorian print, I needed to know how many other fabrics

I would need, and how much of each of these fabrics. To do that, I needed to settle on a pattern. I considered several possibilities before discovering one I liked.

In the March/April 2002 issue of *Quiltmaker* magazine, I found a simple pattern consisting of large squares alternating with pairs of rectangles, each half the size of the squares, inspired by floor tiles. This seemed a good way to show off the detailed print that would be lost if it were cut into smaller pieces.

The pattern gave me the yardage I'd need for three more fabrics. The pattern designer, Andrea Gurdon of Romeo, Michigan, named her quilt Courtyard. I decided to make a few changes in her design to use up some more of those 5 yards of fabric. I will probably refer to my quilt as Love Letters because of the fabric, but I will consider it to be a Courtyard pattern since that is what Ms. Gurdon named it.

Several weeks after I started carrying a swatch of the Victorian fabric in my purse, I found my first match, a tiny rose print on a black background. I had been considering rose prints but had expected to get roses on white or cream, figuring these would be the most likely to complement the love letters since they were the dominant feature on the fabric and composed of tiny black letters on gold-edged cream pages. If I had been too set on the expected, I wouldn't have tested my swatch against some darker fabrics. When I did, I discovered that behind the roses and curling letters, the background of my fabric was, in fact, black. The combination of the two fabrics is more elegant than either is alone.

Now there were two fabrics in my bag. Enough roses, I thought. The next should be something cream and gold to complement the love letters. Perhaps the fourth fabric should be a tone on tone blue to match the slivers of blue print that peek out from behind some of the letters; little blue envelopes, I suppose.

I've found the blue, a better match than I ever expected, but I'm still searching for the last color.

I've nearly bought cream-colored fabrics that I ultimately decided were too boring. I considered a gold and white star print that was the perfect color but decided the stars were too large to coordinate with the delicate print. I'm willing to be patient; I have other quilts to make. I'm also willing to consider that the perfect fabric may not be what I expect. I'll try to be alert to other possibilities.

Be Present in the Present

Janie Rees has reason to be grateful she was alert to possibilities in the winter of 1988. She tells her story on *Gathered in Time* (Salt Lake City: KUED, 1997), a videotape based on the book *Gathered in Time: Utah Quilts and Their Makers, Settlement to 1950* (University of Utah Press, 1997), by Kae Covington.

Janie had gone to spend a couple of weeks with her parents and noticed a faded pink quilt her parents had thrown over a car they had parked on the street for the winter. The worn-out 9-Patch wasn't what caught her attention. It was the glimpses of a brighter red she saw every time she walked by.

She asked her parents if she might have the quilt, and she took it inside for a better look. Once it had thawed out, she began taking it apart and discovered a 1900-era red and black Shoo Fly quilt underneath. An example of the Shoo Fly pattern is pictured at the beginning of this chapter.

Janie's mother speculated that Janie's great-grandmother, Minnie Colgrove Ashby, had made the older quilt. The colors were still bright, and at first glance, the quilt seemed to be in excellent condition. A closer inspection revealed that it had been mended several times and part of the binding had been replaced. In a few places, fabric had worn through to reveal the batting beneath.

In the 1930s, Janie's grandmother had deemed the quilt too worn for use and had used it as batting for a pastel 9-Patch, which, during the following fifty-plus years, had become worn-out as well.

I wish the grandmother's 9-Patch could have been saved somehow, but it protected the older Shoo Fly quilt until it could be rediscovered and treasured. The 9-Patch was clearly an "everyday quilt" so perhaps the family has some of the quilter's "good quilts" in their trunks or on their guest beds.

What if Janie had never bothered to look at the old blanket that had been thrown over the car? How easy it would have been to walk past it, her mind on other things, and never have registered the glimpse of red. Her mother had taken the serviceable quilt at face value and never bothered to look beneath the surface of the familiar quilt. Janie could have as well.

I may never discover a 100-year-old quilt, no matter how alert I try to be, but early in 2002, an opportunity came my way that, under different circumstances, I might have dismissed.

It was the last day of January, and it had snowed the night before. Evening rain had left patches of ice on sidewalks and pavement and coated tree branches. The light snow hid the dangerous ice beneath, making driving hazardous. With care, I could have made it the twelve miles into work. The highway and our country road were probably safer than the streets in town, which all my coworkers managed to negotiate. But my order from a quilting catalog had arrived a couple of days before. I called in and asked for the day off.

I was eager to begin my first Watercolor quilt. Watercolor is a type of quilt made from small squares, usually measuring 2 inches × 2 inches, which blend into one another. The finished quilt is normally a wall hanging and may be abstract or representational. They are called Watercolor quilts because they sometimes resemble watercolor paintings.

I had been planning a Watercolor quilt for nearly a year and had sketched out an outline of what I hoped to do, a stylized Rocky Mountain scene inspired by several family vacation photos. Born and raised on the Kansas plains, I am exhilarated by the magnitude of the Rockies, the wildness of the mountain forests, the lofty peaks, and sheer cliffs, as well as the intriguing history of mountain men and gold seekers. At the same time, the mountains are restful to me. I go there on vacation, living at a slower pace for a few days. I decided I wanted to try to reproduce a portion of those feelings for my living room.

My catalog order included a sheet of heavy flannel about 45 inches square to make a giant flannel board for a wall. Pieces of fabric will stick to flannel the way the felt-backed pictures stuck to the old flannel boards that grade school teachers used to use to tell stories. The wall of flannel allows a quilter to arrange and rearrange pieces, and then stand back to see how a hanging will look from across the room.

On this self-declared Snow Day, I hung the flannel on the wall of Eden's room, which has become an annex to my much smaller sewing room. She doesn't mind, being a quilter herself. I turned her old student desk into a cutting table and began the task of going through my scrap boxes. Any likely fabric went first to the ironing board, then to the desk, and then up on the flannel.

All kinds of forgotten fabrics turned up during my search. I found green from a skirt an older sister had made in the 1950s and blues from dresses I'd made a decade or so later. A scrap left over from an apron my husband's grandmother had made for me (I inherited her scrap box) and leftover kitchen curtain material also made their way into the design taking shape on the wall.

By late afternoon, my mountain scene was outlined, though far from being completely filled in, Eden's floor was covered with piles of fabric, and my nose was running from the dust the cardboard boxes had not kept away from my fabric. It had been a very satisfying process.

I was about to quit for the day when my literary agent called. A nonfiction publisher she likes to work with was

looking for published authors to write books on various subjects for one of their series. She had given me similar calls
before, and I had not been interested. I'm a novelist—if not by
profession (my fiction publisher dropped me in 1999), then at
least by inclination—and nonfiction had never appealed to me.
I've always listened to the subjects when my agent called,
though, just in case.

As she read through her list, I began writing them down. At
one point, I quit listing and simply underlined the last word I'd
written. Quilting.

I immediately recognized an unexpected opportunity. Not
so much the opportunity to write again, to publish, to get paid
(all great, of course), but the opportunity to learn more about a
subject that fascinated me. However, I was still reluctant to try
my hand at nonfiction. If I had not spent the day quilting, I
might not have had the courage to say yes to the opportunity.

Arthur Miller said, "He who understands everything about
his subject cannot write it. I write as much to discover as to
explain." That is a wonderfully Zen statement and is true, in a
sense, of any creative endeavor—not just writing. Or quilting. It
illustrates my feelings about writing *The Everything*® *Quilting
Book* for Adams Media. I certainly wasn't an expert on quilting
when I started, nor am I now for that matter, but I discovered so
much because I was open to the possibility of writing something
different.

It also illustrates my feeling every time I try a new quilt pattern. I don't start the quilt because I know how to make it; I start
it because I want to learn how to make it. How do I sew 500

little squares together into a Watercolor quilt without getting them out of order or driving myself crazy? The trick is to iron the pieces to fusible interfacing and sew whole rows together at one time. Quilt making becomes an exercise in being willing to look at unexpected possibilities. The right and left sides of the brain, yin and yang, and alertness are all at work.

Quiltscapes

And my Watercolor quilt? It's finished and hangs in our living room. I'm proud of it and enjoy it, though I don't think it conveys more than a fraction of what I intended. My sky works better than my mountain, I think, but that doesn't matter.

My favorite part is the tiny moose cut from a fat quarter I bought in a fabric store way up in the mountains in Leadville, Colorado. He seems to be the focal point of the quilt for me, but I've had to point him out to a few people. Maybe they think a moose in the middle of a wall hanging is too odd to even acknowledge, I don't know.

I do know that the quilt makes me remember all the things I love about the mountains, and in that respect, it's a fulfillment of my vision, however imperfect it may be. And perhaps the notion that I can do better is one of the things that keeps me quilting.

You could say my Watercolor quilt is a landscape painting done with cloth rather than paint. Rebecca Barker, a Cincinnati, Ohio, artist, does the opposite. Since 1994 she has been painting quilts that are so realistic I want to touch the cloth. In her earlier paintings, quilts hang on clotheslines, but in her more recent works, the quilts themselves become part of and blend into the landscape. She calls these paintings Quiltscapes.

In an article in the April 2002 issue of *American Patchwork and Quilting*, Rebecca Barker says she was inspired by her great-great-grandmother whose 1894 quilt hangs in her home. She's made quilts, too, but can paint them faster. She has painted more than 350. Besides selling the original paintings, she has a line of products—such as note cards, puzzles, coasters, and calendars—that feature her paintings. Her products sell in quilt shops and at quilt shows. Quilters love her work, of course, but nonquilters are attracted to the peace and beauty of her somewhat romanticized version of rural life.

Rebecca compares painting to quilting, saying they are both "peaceful and relaxing." The peace she finds in painting, her need for creativity, and her connection to the past are all things she has in common with quilters.

She says she finds inspiration not only in the old quilt patterns she uses in her paintings but in quilters that she meets at quilt shows. Interesting that she would find us inspiring when her paintings do so much for us. Besides inspiring us to try the patterns she connects with homey scenes and nature, she affirms quilts themselves as an art form. They are more than just charming. They are beautiful enough for her to let them dominate her paintings.

It's easy for us to call Rebecca Barker a true artist. After all, she has a fine arts degree and makes a living from her paintings.

It's a little harder sometimes to see our own creative efforts as worthy of the title *art*.

But why? Let's consider a dictionary-style definition: Art is a work produced by the conscious use of skill and creative imagination. I think our quilts qualify.

If you're alert, you'll notice how other artists and illustrators use quilts or quilt designs. I've seen quilt patterns on note cards (though not always as accurately depicted as in Rebecca Barker's paintings), on vinyl tablecloths, clothes, china dishes, photo album covers (perfect for quilt diaries), novel covers, and, of course, as fabric prints. Proof, to my way of thinking, that quilts are works of art.

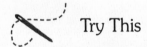 Try This

Make a Watercolor quilt. Sketch a vaguely representational image of something that has personal relevance for you. Think less about how the finished hanging will look in your house and more about what creating this particular hanging will mean. What settings or activities get you excited? Which ones bring you peace? And which are you more in need of right now?

Use your sketch as a starting guide, but don't be afraid to stray from it. Collect fabrics that appeal to you and find a way to use them in your quilt. If the gray and pink kitten print looks nothing like the grass in your imagination but makes you think of how the grass felt, find a way to use it anyway. It doesn't matter if no one else looking at your quilt can see what inspired you.

chapter two

Commit Yourself to the Task

Cutting the Pieces

Accuracy is important when you cut your pieces. Iron your prepared fabric so wrinkles don't interfere. An acrylic ruler and rotary cutter on a specially made cutting pad are easiest, but you can use a yardstick, pencil, and scissors. Curves and odd shapes call for templates. Make your own out of cardboard, and draw around them on your fabric. If you are machine piecing, add ¼-inch seam allowances all around your pattern before you cut the template and mark the cutting line on your fabric. If you are hand piecing, cut your template to the finished shape, mark the stitching line on your fabric, and cut approximately ¼ inch outside the markings.

Quilting for Confidence

A music teacher who played and taught many instruments was asked which instrument was the most difficult to learn. "The first" was his reply. While my first quilt wasn't really the most difficult to make, it was definitely the most difficult to begin.

My husband, Joe, and I were expecting our first child when I decided to make a nongender-specific baby quilt. I shouldn't have been particularly worried about doing it. I had been sewing since my early teens, earlier if you count hand-stitched doll clothes. But this was to be my first quilt. There seemed to be a certain mystery or mystique to the whole quilting thing. Besides, this was also going to be my first baby and my desire to have everything perfect may have made me hesitate.

A few months earlier while making curtains for our bedroom, I had mismeasured the length of one of the panels and had cut it 1 foot too short. I realized the mistake immediately, while the fabric pieces were still lying on the floor in front of me. I remember thinking that I suddenly understood why my sister Nora liked to cook more than she liked to sew. If the fabric had been piecrust, I could have sprinkled it with water and pressed the pieces back together. There was no such easy solution to my sliced fabric.

It was Sunday and the fabric store was closed, leaving me to ponder possible solutions instead of actually making my curtains. A seam to correct my mistake would have been highly visible across one curtain, especially when daylight shone through it. I considered several options such as covering the seam with some type of trim and, of course, sewing the same trim across the other panel. How would this strip of trim look 12 inches from the top? How about 12 inches from the bottom? Neither seemed very attractive. Also, I couldn't imagine what kind of trim would look good on textured blue double knit. (Yeah, you guessed it. It was the 1970s.)

In the end I was able to find more of the same fabric and cut out a new curtain. Since then, I have mismeasured and miscut several times, and clearly the world has not come to an end. But at age twenty, when I decided to make that first quilt, the curtain disaster was still fresh in my mind. The guilt over the added expense, the frustration of a Sunday afternoon free to sew but unable to, and the embarrassment of discovering I wasn't the great seamstress I thought I was were not yet things to laugh about. I wanted to make a quilt for my baby, but I didn't actually know how to do it, and, with my confidence shaken, I was afraid to begin.

I put off the actual construction of the quilt by embroidering pictures taken from a coloring book onto the blocks. Embroidery was familiar to me, and I did not hesitate to begin that phase of the project. When I had six little pigtailed and straw-hatted farm kids with animals outlined in colorful embroidery floss on the blocks, I had to learn how to make a quilt.

The baby's due date may have helped move me forward. A greater nudge was provided by my husband's purchase of a simple quilt frame from a catalog store. It wasn't so much the fact that I now had a frame and needed to put it to use, as it was the realization that my young husband seemed to think

I could make a quilt, and I didn't want to disappoint him. The only thing to do was jump in.

Making that first slice into the pale yellow fabric committed both the fabric and me to that particular quilt. My daughter, Eden, talks about her hesitancy to begin cutting out her first quilt.

She had an inherited 1967 Singer sewing machine when I started writing *The Everything® Quilting Book,* and she was acting as my first reader while finishing the last courses for her master's degree. Postponing working on her thesis, she decided to try out the "antique" sewing machine and start a small project from my book. She began with the idea of making a Log Cabin potholder.

She was very nervous about cutting the first pieces. What if she made mistakes she wouldn't know how to fix? Was it all going to be a waste of money and time?

As she put off taking the plunge into her project, she continued to collect fat quarters, those precut and daintily folded lengths of fabric 18 inches by half a fabric width. Like nearly all quilters, she became addicted to them. As a result, her plans kept expanding to accommodate her growing collection of fabric. The longer she put off beginning, the more she became afraid that some new, better plan might come to mind, and it would be too late to consider it if her pieces were already cut.

"That first cutting was like breaking the ice," she says. "There's a big tension buildup in the planning and acquiring of the fabric. I just had to dive in to build up my confidence."

Reminding herself that there would be other quilts helped allay her fears. When she finally committed herself to a project for all those fat quarters, she made a queen-size 9-Patch quilt. She laughs now that she was even procrastinating about beginning her procrastination project.

It takes some courage to fight down the impulse to second-guess yourself. Should I choose this pattern or that? This size or that? This arrangement or that? Either will be fine. Perhaps a clear understanding of your purpose will help you overcome your fear of beginning.

There Will Be Other Quilts

Right purpose is another of the keys to happiness mentioned in the last chapter. If your purpose for making a quilt, or your purpose for doing anything for that matter, is clear to you, it's easier to commit yourself to the task. And you are less likely to become distracted or swayed by cutting remarks once you are committed to your project. Well-meaning fabric store clerks can offer advice that serves only to shake the already tenuous confidence of beginners. Friends are often quick to tell a new quilter about the quilt they started years ago and never finished, leaving a beginner to wonder why she should be any different. Rest assured, there are plenty of people around who finish one quilt after another. If you want to make a quilt and are confident in your purpose, you'll be one of those who finish.

The late Darrel Silkman, our local Presbyterian pastor some fifteen years ago, liked to say that if something fulfills its true purpose, it is perfect. He was usually speaking of a church dinner that had been attended by only a few members. If those who came enjoyed food and fellowship, the dinner had fulfilled its purpose and hence had been perfect. If the organizers measured the event's success by attendance numbers, they were disappointed, but only because they had lost sight of its true purpose.

As a quilting example, if your purpose for trying a difficult pattern, such as the Lone Star pictured at the beginning of this chapter, is to learn how this type of quilt is done, then it doesn't matter if a few details don't quite turn out the way the instructions say they should. In fact, you'll learn the most from the steps that give you trouble. You don't have to hurry through the process. Since you admit that you're learning, you can expect it to take some time. If you keep your purpose in mind, you can relax and enjoy the process.

If your purpose is to make a baby quilt for a friend to wrap her child in, does it matter if it's a simple block quilt instead of a fancy appliqué? Not to the baby, certainly, and probably not to the mother either. Your love for the family will be present in the quilt and overshadow any crooked seam, puckered binding, or oversized stitches. The quilt will serve its purpose and will be perfect by Darrel's definition.

A quilt intended to match your bedroom colors and keep you warm at night doesn't need to be pieced and stitched with enough precision to win first place in a quilt show. On the other hand, if your purpose for making a particular quilt *is* the blue ribbon, I hope you look at it as a challenge to improve your skills, to push yourself toward a personal best. You'll have a knockout quilt when the show's over. If you're after the challenge, you can congratulate yourself on what you've learned and accomplished and look for ways to use these new skills in the next project, whether you win or not.

The blue-ribbon purpose would not feel like the right one to me, but it might to you. If that ribbon becomes more important than the quilt, however, you ought to ask yourself if all the quilts in the show are failures except the one with the grand prize. Nobody attending the show is going to think so. You need to lighten up a little and jump in for the fun.

In fact, there was a superstition in the eighteenth and nineteenth centuries that a structurally perfect quilt would bring bad luck to the quilter. To avoid this curse, one piece on the face of the quilt would intentionally be cut from the wrong color of fabric or one block would be turned upside down, thus disrupting the continuity of the pattern. To strive for perfection was to rival God, the quilters believed.

I have never worried about my quilts being too perfect. They have enough errors without my making any intentional ones. On that first baby quilt, my quilting stitches are very large and uneven. The rows of stitches are too far apart, besides. If I had used it more and washed it more, the batting would probably have pulled apart and bunched up here and there. Before I pass it on to another generation, I really ought to put it back in the frame and add about twice as many stitches as are in it now. My current stitches wouldn't match those old ones. Besides, the quilt has already fulfilled its purpose, and I would have more fun making something new.

To Have and to Hold

Every quilter has a first quilt, and most remember it with fond-ness mixed with some degree of embarrassment for the quality of that first effort. This may be a source of the tradition that says you should keep your first quilt. It would be better to try a few more and improve your skill before you start giving them away. Also, if you keep that first one, you can use it to measure all future quilts against. Most quilters remember as well what brought them to begin that first quilt. Several other quilters I talked to recalled making their first quilts for their first child. There seems to be a little of the nesting instinct at work here, as we teach ourselves quilting out of a desire to have these quilts for our babies.

My sister Nancy Jones embroidered pictures from a coloring book—in this case, nursery rhyme pictures—on her first quilt. I was about eight years old when her first child was born. I may very well have seen and liked that quilt, and then stole the idea years later without remembering where it came from. Nancy says she remembers quilting as being fun. She made two or three quilts before time and other factors kept her from it for many years, and she hasn't gone back into it. Yet.

My friend Nancy Collins made her first quilt for her first baby. She says she wasn't hesitant to begin it because she didn't care if it wasn't very professional. "It's still together, at least," she says of that first quilt, which is stored away somewhere. She's recently come back to quilting or, as she puts it, is beginning "real" quilting now that she's retired and has more time to sew.

By real quilting, she means she's doing more elaborate piecing and appliqué, but primarily she means she's quilting the layers together instead of tying them as she did her first quilt. Calling her recent projects "real quilting" gives her an excuse to chart her progress from the beginning of these more recent quilts, which benefit from years of other sewing.

Another friend I'll call Linda made her first quilt for a baby, too, this time for her first grandchild. She is related to an avid quilter who made her think she ought to try it. Linda chose a paper-pieced pattern, thinking it would give her a guide. Unfortunately, paper piecing is usually designed to keep the quilter accurate when piecing a very complicated design. The pattern is printed on paper and you sew the pieces directly onto the paper, following the printed lines. The paper is torn away later. Linda's pattern was even trickier than most, featuring little pieced people in a row. She finished the quilt but says she doesn't care to ever do one again.

I'm hoping my friend will reconsider. A first quilt is, after all, a first. Not only does that imply that a second should follow, but it suggests a measure of forgiveness is in order. Linda is very artistic and perhaps the fact that she has several other creative outlets (like painting, which I couldn't do in my dreams) keeps her from being drawn back to quilting. Left to make up her own designs, she would no doubt make some very imaginative quilts. I would love to see them.

Joyce Swenson refers to her first quilt as a shot in the dark. Her purpose was also the finished quilt, although her reasons were different. She had always wanted an antique quilt and kept wishing some distant aunt or other relative would pass one on to her. She finally decided that was never going to happen. If she wanted a quilt, she was going to have to make it herself. At the time, she couldn't find anyone to teach her how and, like several of us, learned as she went along. She started with something simple, she says, but will tackle about anything now. She had made several quilts before she found some classes. She loves discovering new techniques for doing things she has been doing the hard way.

Nancy Chaffee Parker was in high school when she made her first quilt. She made it for a bedspread to take with her to college. She doesn't remember being hesitant to begin even though she hadn't sewn very much. Her purpose was also the quilt itself. She made exactly what she wanted and loved it, she says. At this point in her quilting endeavors, she neither remembers nor cares how technically imperfect that first quilt might have been. It did exactly what it was supposed to do: It kept her warm, brightened her room, and made her feel confident. It was a perfect quilt.

Like me, these quilters and many others began their first quilt out of a desire for the finished product. Those of us who have continued to quilt, or in some cases returned to it, have probably made more quilts than we really need. After a while, the process became more important than the product and our purpose changed.

A Little Push

Some quilters have had help taking the plunge into quilt making. Marguerite Martin began her first quilt when she was a teenager. Her purpose had little to do with any real desire to learn to quilt. She was a farm girl, and one winter around 1930, she lived with a family in town while she attended high school. In the evening "instead of getting to walk up and down the streets with the other young folks," she and the daughter of the house each hand pieced a Lone Star quilt. She must not have been too disappointed in this turn of events because she refers to her temporary guardian as a "dear lady."

A Lone Star quilt is made up of several hundred diamond-shaped pieces all the same size. A small version of the pattern is illustrated at the beginning of this chapter. Marguerite's, like many Lone Stars, was made in the colors of the spectrum beginning with red in the center. The project took the girls most of the winter. In 1930, she might have been sewing by lamp-light, gaslight, or even electric lights, depending on the location and the prosperity of the family, but most likely she was snug and warm. Her friends downtown were probably not having as much fun out on the windy streets of the small northern Kansas town as she imagined. Marguerite's purpose for stitching all those diamonds together was obedience, which may well have been stressed by her parents before she left home. It's easy to understand the "dear lady's" purpose. She had the responsibility of keeping a young girl out of trouble, and what better way to do it than to keep her busy? But she also taught young Marguerite a lifelong skill. "It was a joy," Marguerite says, "working on something useful that would last a long time."

At ninety-one, Marguerite no longer quilts. Her sister-in-law finished Marguerite's last effort when her eyesight became too poor to quilt. She misses it, she says. It would help to pass the time.

And her first quilt? She thought a lot of that quilt and treasured it, but during the Great Depression she and her husband needed to use it. Use and repeated washings finally wore it out. She still has it, though, hidden, like Janie Rees's great-grandmother's quilt, inside another.

Some quilters make their first quilt as part of a class or church group. The support and fellowship of other quilters, not to mention the instruction, give them confidence.

Teresa LaFlair's first quilt was made for a class she attended to please her daughter, not out of any desire to learn to quilt. It was a Fence Rail made from fabrics with stars and moons. She hadn't cared a lot for the fabric, but it was what her daughter liked, and she was making it for her. At the time, her daughter was dating a boy who had a younger sister with cerebral palsy. The younger sister was often at the house and fell in love with the quilt. When she wanted to take it home with her, Teresa and her daughter decided to let her keep it.

Teresa said she heard later about the tradition of keeping your first quilt, but had she heard of it sooner, she would still have done the same thing.

A quilter who asked to be identified only as Bonnie went to her first quilting class with a coworker. She had never sewn as a girl because her mother was an avid seamstress. Bonnie's mother could make anything and do it so quickly that she and her sisters never really got a chance to sew. Bonnie was a bit skeptical when she came to the first class, but the atmosphere won her over. The walls were decorated with the teacher's quilts, soft music was playing, and all the other students were quick to encourage each other. If this calm and friendly atmosphere was quilting, she wanted to be part of it.

Clearly Bonnie's mother hadn't intended to discourage her daughters from sewing. It was probably just easier to do it herself than teach her daughters how, especially with a large family to care for. When Bonnie and her mother were dining out one day, they met Bonnie's instructor. Mom thanked her, saying, "Out of four daughters, I finally have one who sews."

Beginner's Mind

The quilters I talked to were about evenly divided between people who had done a lot of sewing before they made their first quilt and those who had done next to none. Experience doesn't seem to have any bearing on how hesitant they were to begin that first quilt. Even for some of the people who liked to sew, the first quilt seemed like a giant step into the unknown. If you have never done any sewing, don't let that discourage you. If you have been sewing all your life, you might want to cultivate a beginner's mind.

In Zen practice, you attempt to experience life without the intrusion of all your opinions, ideas, and beliefs, to live here and now with the way things really are. This isn't easy to do. It can take a long time to learn to be a beginner.

With the confidence of youth, Marsha Wentz made a set of quilt blocks when she was in junior high school. She had been sewing since she was a little girl making doll clothes. Catherine Silhan was also in junior or senior high when she made her first quilt. Both her grandmothers quilted, so for her it was the natural thing to do.

Try to approach your next quilt with the eagerness and innocence that Marsha and Catherine must have had. Set aside all self-criticism and all expectations for the finished product; do it for the doing alone. If you can even have a few moments of seeing your fabric and your quilting with new eyes, you'll understand the beginner's mind.

Pincushion Projects

For some quilters, that first quilt was simply something else to sew. Little did they know that that project would turn them into avid quilters.

Sister Betty Suther began her first quilt as busywork. At the time, her job required a great deal of traveling. She could easily take a sewing basket with her and hand piece a quilt in motel rooms at night. Quilting became an addiction, she says. She now leads two quilting retreats a year at the Manna House of Prayer where she is the administrator. She and other sisters have a quilt in their frame nearly all the time. Often they donate the quilts to charities. Other times, they are quilting someone else's pieced quilt. Still, it's not the pay but the joy of quilting that brings the sisters to the frame.

Marge Eaton says her first quilts were just sewing projects, but now quilts are about all the sewing she does. She lives with her quilts all around her: on the bed, tables, walls, and couch. She says the little ones fit her attention span. She doesn't remember her very first quilt but remembers buying appliqué kits and putting them together. "It was like cutting out paper dolls," Marge says. Now that's a good childish attitude to take.

Barbara Booth began quilting because of a sewing project she inherited. Barbara's great-great-grandmother had pieced three quilt tops when she was over 100 years old. The tops were eventually handed down to Barbara who quilted them. It became a sharing experience with her mother. Barbara would quilt and her mother would talk about the women of the family, like the ancestor who had worked in a shirt factory in Chicago and had survived the Chicago fire by finding shelter under a bridge. Barbara knows a lot more about the lives of her foremothers than she ever would have if it hadn't been for the quilts.

Kathryne Perney says she *needs* to sew. Her first quilt was begun shortly after her marriage. They didn't have any money to buy fabric, but she needed a sewing project. She pieced scraps together, giving her a chance to sew without spending any money. She used a thermal blanket for batting and tied it because she didn't know how to quilt. What she considers her first "real" quilt, the first one she quilted, was made for the same reason. She didn't need any clothes and her sons didn't need anything, yet she needed to sew.

Potluck Projects

Several quilters mentioned making their first quilt in an effort to use up fabric left over from other sewing projects. My own second attempt to make a full-size quilt was begun for this reason. It's a Cathedral Window, which uses tiny squares of lots and lots of fabrics. Unfortunately, I made more leftovers from other projects faster than I used them up on that still-unfinished quilt.

Other quilters had better luck. My favorite story along this line is from Cindy Kahrs. Her husband had given her a sewing machine shortly after they were married. She used it a little but not much. When they were expecting their first child, Cindy bought a pattern to make a bunting and showed it to her mother. Her mother gave her two large boxes of fabric left over from her own sewing projects, hoping that Cindy could use some of it to make baby clothes.

Unfortunately most were scraps too small to make clothes for a baby, and Cindy stored the boxes away. She and her family lived in a small trailer house at the time with very limited storage space. Cindy felt a need to start using up the fabric because the boxes were taking up too much room! (She was meant to be a quilter or she would have just thrown the scraps away, don't you think?)

At the checkout line at the grocery store, a quilting magazine with a picture of a 9-Patch quilt on the cover caught her eye. She decided that was what she would do with the fabric. By this time their daughter was around ten months old. Cindy would put her sewing machine on the kitchen table with her daughter on her right in a playpen and the ironing board with the scissors and pins on her left out of the baby's reach. By the time the day was over, the playpen would be full of fabric the little girl had pulled off the table. "We both had a blast!" she says.

She used a sheet for the backing and a blanket for the batting and hemmed the edge rather than encasing it in binding. "An experienced quilter would have had a good laugh at that quilt, but at the time I thought I'd done a pretty good job," she says.

And what happened to the quilt? They used it for several years; then it was stolen. Cindy's husband is a custom harvester, and she travels with him from Texas to North Dakota, cooking for him and his crew. They stay in one camper and house the employees in another. She put the quilt in the employees' camper and one of them took it home. "Apparently someone else liked it more than I did," she adds.

In case you're wondering if early exposure to playing with fabric turned the little girl in the playpen into a quilter, I'm happy to tell you it did but not right away. Kristy J. Kahrs was too busy with music in high school to be interested in quilting. It wasn't until she had moved away that she took some quilting classes. She says she needed a hobby, but I suspect she was homesick. What better way to bring back a feeling of home than to make your new home feel a little like your old one? Quilting may have been the sewing equivalent of getting Mom's apple pie recipe.

Purposeful Projects

Sarah Croco, a friend of my daughter's, has her reasons for beginning a quilt all thought out; she just hasn't started it yet. When she e-mailed me with her point-by-point list, she was hoping for a sewing machine for her birthday. Nobody in her family has ever made a quilt, but she's ready to be the first. "The main reason is that I really like to make gifts for people, but I haven't had much luck with other crafts."

At one time Eden had tried to teach her to knit. Evidently Sarah had never gotten the hang of it. "I always had to have Eden there in case I dropped a stitch," she writes. She just couldn't make it work and was frustrated by the slow progress. "I already know how to work a sewing machine, so I think I have the required entry-level skill." Sarah figures she "can just go a piece at a time and little mistakes won't be so noticeable in the final project." I think her enthusiasm is going to serve her at least as well as her skill with a sewing machine.

Another skill she's already developed is shopping. "I've always loved fabric stores and I think going through all the fabrics and selecting some for a quilt would be lots of fun." Most of all, she's looking forward to making quilts as gifts, tailoring them to particular people in terms of color and pattern, and sewing each quilt with a particular person in mind.

I'm looking forward to hearing how it all goes for her.

Getting to Know You

Many quilters expressed their pleasure at seeing that first quilt through to the end. I remember feeling relieved that it didn't take as long to quilt as I expected. But then, I only quilted it about a third as much as I should have. Still, the second and third quilts were easier. That first quilt was a special experience. For many of them, a quilt hadn't seemed like something they could do. There may have been several times during the course of making it when failure seemed a possibility. But those of us who stayed with it to the end usually have the courage to try it again. And that second quilt isn't nearly as difficult to begin.

My daughter calls making her first quilt empowering. She hadn't done much sewing of any kind prior to this project. I'm not sure I would necessarily recommend a queen-size quilt as a first sewing project, but the secret was that it was something she really wanted to make. She was willing to plunge in and try it because she wanted it badly enough. Until she took that first step, she had decided making a quilt would be impossible. "Turns out," she says, "it's all a lot easier than I thought." What other seemingly impossible feats is she going to be willing to tackle now?

Maybe you haven't tackled that first quilt because of pre-conceived notions of how it has to be done. Try to have a beginner's mind and take the plunge. If you've made several quilts, think about how you approached the process. A primary aim of Zen is to know yourself and looking at your quilting style can be a form of self-examination. How do *you* begin a quilt? Are you organized and methodical: one fabric at a time, largest pieces first, conserving as much of the fabric as possible? This may mean you intend to make a lot of quilts and you don't want to waste time later sorting or searching. You may notice that you're organized in other areas of your life as well.

Do you cut passionately for hours one day and not return to the task for weeks? This might indicate that you have a variety of interests, or a shortage of time for your hobby. Or do you approach other tasks and even relationships with similar swings between passion and neglect?

Do you begin with the primary fabric of your quilt or with whatever fabric interests you today? Do you follow a set of directions very carefully or do you glance at the directions for a general idea and only return to them if you find yourself stuck? Your answers might tell you if you are led by emotion or logic, if you feel a need for guidelines or enjoy the freedom of winging it.

Perhaps you'll discover your approach to quilting is the opposite of your approach to work, relationships, and other aspects of your life. Maybe quilting is the one thing you *can* keep organized, or the one place you are free to improvise. Only you can figure that out.

If you have not begun your first quilt, you can't answer these questions, but you can ask yourself why you are resisting. Is your purpose unclear? Do you lack confidence? If you could begin any way you wanted to, which, of course, you can, how would you do it?

I usually have a few projects in the works at any given time. This gives me a chance to choose what I feel like doing at the moment I have some quilting time. I can sit and appliqué my Dresden Plate blocks or machine piece that new sunflower fabric for a quilt for my younger son Paul's bed. Often I have quilting and piecing projects to work on as well. However, I have the luxury of a sewing space where I can leave my work-in-progress from one sewing session to the next. There are no children or pets in my house, so scissors and pins left sitting out are no longer a concern. If all your cutting gear and fabric must be gathered off the kitchen table before the next meal, you will probably be forced to be more organized than I am. If you don't have a sewing room, maybe all you need is a sewing closet or a sewing shelf. Store things in stacking tubs to save space. Label your pieces when you pick them up in case you've forgotten just where you are by the time you get your project out again. If your sewing time is limited, you don't want to spend half of it trying to reorganize so you can begin.

We all need a place to work as well as a place to store our supplies. We might need to change our thinking about the traditional use of a room and set up our sewing in a corner of the bedroom or living room. A clamp-type light that can be stored away with other supplies might make a space usable that would otherwise be rejected. Be creative in finding your sewing space.

Remember, a hundred and fifty years ago, women living in one-room cabins still managed to make quilts. They hung quilt frames from the ceiling so they could raise them out of the way. They tucked their basket of quilt pieces under the bed by day and probably did the daily mending first in the evening before getting back to their quilts. The trailer Cindy Kahrs was living in when she made her first quilt was probably nearly as crowded.

Time is another factor probably more difficult to deal with than space. Few of us really *have* time for any hobby until we decide to *make* time for it. Sharon Fields, a quilting instructor, says that, while she had always sewn, she never figured she'd have time to make a quilt. Finally she just decided to do it. This is essentially what we all end up doing. Our natural urge toward creativity finally overwhelms our practical side and we begin.

If your purpose is clear to you and right for you, you'll find the space and the time and the courage to get started. Eventually, the right method will come, too. And who knows what it will tell you about yourself.

What you learn may not be monumental, but we all ought to have the fun of getting to know ourselves better. One of the things I've learned about myself through a quilt-cutting experience is that I tend to put off the difficult part and do the easy things first. This is probably more lack of confidence than pro-crastination. I tell myself that by the time the easy fabrics are all cut out, I'll know what to do with the difficult one.

The problem with this theory came home to me recently when I picked out a one-way print as my primary fabric for a quilt. The motif on the print turned out to be too large for the squares I needed for the pattern. It simply wouldn't work.

Fortunately, I came to this conclusion after cutting only two or three patches. However, the other two fabrics were all cut out. If I had faced my most difficult challenge first, I could have changed the pattern using larger patches and adjusted every-thing accordingly. By putting it off, I committed the other fabrics to a pattern my picture print wouldn't fit. I decided to put the picture print away and find something else to fit with the fabrics I'd already cut out. I took swatches of my coordinating fabric shopping to find a new primary print.

The second thing I learned about myself is that I can't always muster that patience I wrote about in the last chapter. My pur-pose for making this quilt had already changed and would change again, as it turned out. Originally, I wanted to test my instructions for the 9-Patch described in Appendix A. The two fabrics I'd cut had already accomplished that. Now I wanted to find something to use with those two fabrics I'd already cut out. It had become a salvage operation. And besides that, I wanted the fabric *today*. All those strips and squares stacked in my sewing room had to be dealt with before I could sew anything else, and I was in a mood to sew. I found a sunflower print with a denim blue background. I took it home and spread it out. I put a few of my cut pieces on top of it to simulate the quilt design. And that's when I learned something else. I really miss my younger son, Paul. As I write this, he's with his National Guard unit in Tuzla, Bosnia. I was fabric shopping about three days before his birthday. I'm not sure why the sunflower print made me think of him. Maybe because he's a Kansas boy a long way from home, and the sunflower is our state flower. More likely, it's because I used his bed to spread out the fabrics. Whatever it was, I decided the quilt would be for him.

That new purpose changed everything. The quilt had to be better than three sort-of-go-together fabrics. All the motifs were too small. I realized, now that I cared more, that the new sunflower print would look better as the borders and the panels between the blocks if I could just get a larger-scale sunflower print. The original panel material was perfect for the picture print I'd put away so I put it away as well. Whatever I decide to do with it in the future, I'll surely find a use for the white fabric with tiny blue leaves, even though it is mostly cut into narrow strips.

So it was back to the store where I found some cheery sunflowers that were just the right size for the blocks I intended to cut. (I was more conscious of that kind of thing, now. I learn best from my mistakes, but I hate these refresher courses.)

Excited by the prospect of having a new quilt on Paul's bed before he got home from Bosnia, I cut the big sunflowers into squares and cut the smaller print into new panels and borders. I started sewing my squares together for the blocks, but something kept bothering me. A black-and-white-checked fabric.

The next thing I learned about myself is I value the effort I put into a quilt more than the money. I had seen a black-and-white check that was an exact match to the little squares in my border fabric when I was looking for the sunflowers. I couldn't stop thinking about how much better it would look than the blue that hadn't really been bought for *this* quilt anyway. If I intended to spend all that time on a quilt for Paul, I should make it the best possible quilt. I ended up putting the tone-on-tone blue away with the other two fabrics. Paul's quilt will have the black-and-white check along with the sunflowers in the 9-Patch blocks.

Not one fabric in Paul's quilt is what I started with. When I use those three original fabrics, I know there'll be more than the usual amount of waste as I cut them down again to fit a new pattern, but Paul's quilt will be worth it. And the blue quilt will be a better quilt than the one I would have made if I'd gone ahead and cut the picture print into small blocks. So I know I made the right decision to put them away.

I think I am better at picking patterns that are perfect for a fabric than I am at trying to shop for fabric with a particular pattern in mind. That will be something that I'll keep in mind in the future.

I have a few ideas for using those blue fabrics, ideas that will show off the large pictures and use most of the other fabrics. I may call that quilt something like Second Try Treasure or Rejoined Rejects. Or maybe by the time I've finished that quilt, it'll be a quilt on its own enough that it won't seem like a salvage operation at all.

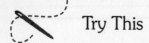 ## Try This

Meditate on your purpose for quilting the next time you're strolling through a fabric store, perusing a quilting book, or sorting through your fabric stash. The first thought that comes to your mind might be the reason you believe you *ought* to have. Or perhaps it's the excuse you give an unsympathetic world. Think of several other possible reasons for wanting to make a quilt. You'll know when you discover your true purpose. With your purpose clearly in mind, committing yourself to beginning will come more easily.

If you've made several quilts, re-examining your purpose for quilting in general and especially for wanting to make a particular quilt will add to your enjoyment of every step.

chapter three

Red and Yellow,
Black and White

Piecing

Straight-edged pieces can be sewn together by machine or by hand. Curved pieces will go together more accurately by hand. Clip inward curves to within a thread or two of the stitching line at 1- to ½-inch intervals, depending on the depth of the curve. Use small running stitches and make sure your needle is on the stitching lines of both pieces before you pull it through. Back stitch or knot the ends of your thread. Press the seam allowances toward the inward curve on curved seams and toward the darker fabric on straight seams whenever practical.

They Are Precious in His Sight

If you've taken the leap and cut out your pieces, you've developed enough confidence to have some faith in the outcome of your project. Or maybe you've just told yourself that whether or not the quilt works out, you will be better for having done it. This, too, is faith. Every quilt is its own experience and seems to develop a personality of its own before it's done. Maybe that's why quilters through history have given them names.

I hand pieced a Charm quilt recently. Charm quilts get their name from magical charms and go back at least to the eighteenth century. The idea is that every piece in the quilt is the same size and shape (making it a One-Patch), but each is of a different fabric. If a single woman collected fabric for a Charm quilt, she was supposed to meet her future husband when she found that last piece. She would probably ask her neighbors for scraps to donate, saving families with eligible sons until the end. Of course, I imagine if she met a man she didn't like about the time she collected what she expected to be the last piece, she would suddenly decide to make her quilt a little larger. The opposite could be true as well. Since superstitions can be surprisingly strong, I would imagine Charm quilts have been made in a variety of sizes.

I wasn't looking for a husband when I made my Charm quilt. In the old days, when married women made the same type of quilts, they called them Beggar quilts because they would beg scraps off their neighbors. I saved my quilt from such an unappealing name by having ample fabric of my own, at least for the lap-robe size I wanted. And, as with any quilt I make, I can call it what I want, so it's my Charm quilt. Besides, the name Charm has stayed popular, while Beggar has been lost to nearly everyone but quilt historians.

Charm quilts can be made into a game for children. A young mother would make two patches of the same fabric and hide them among the others on the quilt. In the days before videogames, children could amuse themselves by trying to find the matching pair.

When I made my Charm quilt, I wanted to try out a Double Axe Head pattern, which is a circle with inverted curves on two quarters that exactly match the outward curves on the other two. The single shape resembles a double-headed ax. It's sometimes called an Apple Core, but when several are sewn together, they look more like overlapping circles. The effect intrigued me and I wanted to try it out, but I was also intent on using up scraps. I was in the middle of sorting through my boxes of fabric and reorganizing it all to make it easier to find what I needed when I needed it.

I cut my pieces from the smallest scraps that would accommodate my pattern first and then moved on to my quarter-yard-or-so collection to get enough different fabrics. It wasn't until I started the slower, hand-piecing step that I really saw the fabric pieces as individuals. Each had its own qualities and its own place in the quilt.

I sat in the evenings, half-watching TV, and sewed the pieces together, one after another. Pin inward curve to outward curve. Line up the stitching lines. Sew them together. Two pieces have become one. Then add another piece. They were nothing but scraps yesterday. Now they are part of a new whole.

We are a little like that, you and I; two separate pieces in the quilt that is humankind. How can we hate or resent or be jealous of someone who is occupying another part of the quilt we're living in? Somehow we manage to. My son Paul is in Bosnia as part of a multinational peacekeeping force. This is an area where groups of people are struggling to realize their place in the region. On a map, what was once one war-torn country is now a patchwork of several nations that haven't stabilized. But there is hope. Paul represents one of many nations working together in the region.

Zen teaches us that God is part of, and running through, all living things. All of us together are one: the Mind of God. Many faiths give voice to similar ideas of connectedness. Unfortunately, some folks extend that oneness only to other folks who hold the same image of God as they do.

However we see God, this piecing of separate fabrics into one quilt cover can get us thinking about how we view other people and faith and our place in it all.

As I pick up a piece of pink and gray gingham to add to my growing Charm quilt, I recognize it as part of Grandma Benson's stash. Minnie Benson was my husband's grand-mother. My own grandmothers had both died before I was born, so Grandma Benson was as close to a grandmother as I ever had. What did she originally buy this fabric for? The color combination makes me think of the 1950s. How far off is my guess? Was it fabric she particularly liked or did she buy it to make something for someone else? What was she thinking when she sewed with this cloth? Was she still on the farm with a growing family, or had she already moved into the little house on Broadway in Concordia?

I recognize a pink-and-blue-flowered print as fabric I bought to make a dress for Eden. For a few years there, most of the fabric I bought was for dresses for my only daughter. I can't remember for sure which dress I made from this fabric. There are a lot of similar scraps. Then she got to be about ten and refused to wear dresses. Now she's in her twenties and asking for help learning to make them for herself.

Here I find a blue-striped fabric I used to make a shirt for my older son Jonathan. I wonder as I stitch it to the rest, how he's doing and picture him for a few minutes as he was at six or seven wearing the shirt with a clip-on necktie. New York City, where he and his wife live while he attends graduate school at New York University studying film, seems a long way away. I quit sewing and give him a call.

Looking back, maybe I should have asked all my sewing friends for fabric for my quilt. It would have given me more people to think about as I sewed. Instead of referring to it as the Charm quilt, I might call it my Friendship quilt.

A Textured Heritage

We tend to think of quilt making as part of Americana, but our innovations are only recent additions to the craft. Quilts were evolving long before the first European woman made her bed in the New World. While quilting isn't exactly a universal pastime (there isn't much need for quilts in the tropics, I suppose), it has been practiced over much of the world. Each culture has added a piece to the huge patchwork that is our quilting heritage.

By definition, quilting is the layering of fabric together. Quilting probably began shortly after weaving was developed, and the first quilts may have been sleeping pallets. Evidence of quilting has been found in ancient villages along the Nile and the Tigris-Euphrates Valley.

Asians refined the process and were quilting garments extensively by the Middle Ages. Crusaders brought some of the Middle Eastern garments home to Europe along with other plunder. The first use in Europe seems to be as padding under the heavy armor the knights wore. This leaves us with rather a violent picture, not exactly the peaceful, homey image we identify with quilts today.

An extremely cold winter in England is credited with the development of quilting as bed coverings. I don't know if that is true, however, because the word *quilt* comes from the Old French word for "mattress," and suggests an early use of the technique as bedding. However, it may be that the process went by some other name until the homemakers of England started making quilted bedding during that particularly cold winter. Perhaps someone said, "That looks like the *cuiltes* I saw in France." Whatever happened exactly, many European cultures contributed to what quilting has become.

In the Middle Ages, England was famous for its exquisite embroidery. The artisans added quilts to their repertoire and embroidered colorful coats-of-arms and detailed hunting scenes and the like on their quilts. The embroidery and tapestry frames were converted to quilt frames and the quilting stitches became more detailed. Although this was the invention of the quilting frame, don't image a medieval quilting bee. The artisans were more like sweatshop laborers, filling an order for a wealthy patron.

I suppose these intricately embroidered English quilts fell out of favor when people started wanting to wash their quilts. The thread of the time wasn't colorfast.

By the early 1900s, there was one colorfast thread: Turkey Red. Embroidery was very popular for other household decorating, and quilt makers began outlining pictures on quilt blocks with this colorfast thread. This type of embroidery became known as redwork, even after a washable blue was developed.

Iron-on transfers had been invented about thirty years earlier, but preprinted squares that were ready to embroider were also available. These blocks cost about a penny apiece and were called penny squares.

In the 1920s, techniques were found to make more threads colorfast, and there is now a rainbow of colorfast thread to choose from. Embroidery has remained popular, often with Victorian themes, like fans and parasols, perhaps harking back to the popularity of embroidery during that era. One of the most beautiful quilts I've ever seen was embroidered with

Victorian-style fans and flowers. It was a new quilt on display at a quilt show in a little country church.

Another country to influence today's quilting was France. During the baroque period, France was known for highly decorated furniture, architecture, and clothing. It was the birthplace of appliqué, which means "to put on." French seamstresses covered their quilt tops with intricate floral designs and curlicues that were cut from other fabrics and carefully turned and sewn in place. Appliqué can still be done the same way it's always been, but sewing machines that can make zigzag stitches make it possible to appliqué much more quickly. My second quilt, made for my second child, has six machine-stitched appliquéd Sunbonnet Sues and Overall Sams. At the time, I didn't know I ought to stop and thank the French for the idea.

An example of how quilting is really pieced together from a lot of traditions is *broderie perse*. This is a French phrase meaning Persian embroidery. Despite its name, the technique developed in England around 1700, although its roots are in French appliqué. It refers to the practice of appliquéing printed motifs cut from one fabric onto another solid cloth. The technique is sometimes called chintz appliqué, which describes it a little better.

Chintz was printed cotton imported to England from India beginning around 1600. The English wool and flax industry influenced Parliament to ban the production or importation of cotton. This ban was eventually lifted in favor of a tax, and as a result, this popular cloth became very expensive. This tax and the previous ban extended to the colonies as well, which irritated the colonists more than the tax on tea, but that's a different story.

In order to use the lovely prints without spending so much money, quilters bought a yard of chintz fabric, cut it up, and spread the pictures across their homespun or linen fabric. These became known as one-yard quilts. I have to wonder if this is how the word *chintzy* came to mean "cheap or stingy."

As the technique became more popular, fabrics were designed and printed especially for it—precursors, in a way, to the fabric now printed to look like patchwork or the preprinted blocks ready to sew together and quilt. These are sometimes known by the rather judgmental name of cheater's quilting.

Italy's contribution to quilting is a technique known as *trapunto*. The word means "embroidery," but it is different from English embroidery. Because of the warmer climate, the Italians had no need for padding in their quilts. Instead, they joined two layers of cloth together with stitches that outlined shapes and with sets of parallel stitches running in fancy curves. They then forced tiny pieces of padding between the threads of the back fabric with a bodkin in order to stuff some of the shapes. They inserted a needle threaded with cord through the back fabric and ran it between the parallel stitching lines to deposit the cord between the two layers of fabric. The effect is a sort of embossed look.

This is an incredibly painstaking process, but the modern technique of stuffed quilts, a descendant of *trapunto*, is easier. A small hole is cut in the lining fabric behind an appliquéd piece and pillow stuffing is poked through the hole. When the top is assembled with the batting and the backing, the cut is hidden inside the quilt. Stuffed appliqué is seen most often in baby quilts and decorated tote bags.

Another type of quilt that has its roots in *trapunto* is the Whole Cloth or Plain quilt. These are quilts in which the top is made from one piece of solid color fabric, often white, black, or indigo blue. The beauty of the quilt comes from the quilting stitches and the shadows and textures they create. This particular style of quilting, first popular in France, though influenced by Italian needlework, is another example of the multinational influence on a quilting style still used today. A small example of Plain quilting is illustrated at the beginning of Chapter 8.

Quilting was brought to the colonies with all these European (and Asian) influences. Colonial women, however, had little time to quilt or make their own contribution to the wealth of styles and techniques. The myth of colonial quilts was actually started in the 1920s when all things colonial were popular. Magazines promoted "colonial designs," which actually only dated back to the last half of the nineteenth century, simply to take advantage of the fad.

Americana

But America did eventually add something to the art of quilting. The pieced quilt is America's primary contribution. The early quilts that were covered with patches evolved into pieced quilts of intentional designs. Each community developed its favorite patterns, and one generation's innovation became the next generation's standard. This growing catalog of patterns eventually contained a contribution from what probably seems like an unlikely source. In the 1800s, the government took Native American children from their homes and put them in boarding schools in an effort to help them learn to fit into a culture that was quickly destroying their own. The boys were taught to farm, and the girls were taught to cook and sew, including quilts. When they went home again, the girls incorporated their own religious symbols into their quilts. The Lone Star quilt is really a variation of the Plains Indians' Morning Star quilt. In much the same way, southwestern Indians have incorporated designs from sand paintings into their quilts. Sand painting is a religious ritual, which involves making an intricate pattern with colored sand. Every detail in the painting has symbolic meaning.

Similarly, slave women, who were so limited in opportunity and resources, invented a quilting technique. Some slave women became very skilled seamstresses, sewing for their master's family. They would help with the quilting, enjoying the colors and designs as much as anyone else. How they must have wished for beautiful quilts for their own families! They collected the long strips of cloth that were trimmed from the backing fabric when it was cut to fit the quilt covers. They rescued the tiny scraps that their wealthy white mistresses deemed too small to use and threw away. The slaves sewed these tiny pieces to the strips of backing and then sewed the strips together to make very colorful quilts. The technique is called string piecing, and a sample of it is illustrated at the beginning of this chapter.

Imagine for a moment wrapping your baby in a quilt made from salvaged scraps. You are a slave and this baby you hold belongs to your owner. You know the life that lies ahead for this child, but still you stitched those tiny pieces together to have something beautiful to greet her with. You love and nurture this child when it might seem kinder to smother her and save her from a life of slavery. Imagine the faith that would take.

Ironically, string pieced quilts closely resemble another American invention begun some ten years after the Civil War, Crazy quilt throws. Used only for decoration on the back of a sofa in the parlor, Crazy quilts were made from odd-shaped pieces of the more expensive fabrics, like velvet and satin, and often richly embroidered. I suspect that the two kinds of quilts had more in common than the seamstresses of the time would have realized, if they had even known about each other. Both were invented as ways of getting the most out of their scraps of fabrics.

Crazy quilts are named after the crazed or cracked look of the finish on Japanese ceramics. American women got their first look at these pieces of asymmetrical art at the Philadelphia Centennial Exposition in 1876. Popular women's magazines of the day incorporated the idea into quilts and Crazy quilting was invented.

To further decorate their expensive scraps, Victorian women used silk thread to embroider along each seam. Often the quilter exhibited every kind of stitch she knew on a single quilt. Tiny pictures were sometimes embroidered on particular pieces.

Any subject dear to the seamstress's heart might be reproduced in miniature. Stitching a spider in its web somewhere on the quilt was supposed to bring the quilter luck.

The Native Hawaiian culture also added its style to quilting tradition. Native Hawaiian artists have developed two quilt techniques. The first involves covering the top of the quilt with one symmetrical appliqué. This appliqué is designed by folding paper in eighths and cutting out a shape, much like cutting a large paper snowflake. Although they might be completely abstract, often the designs represent native plants. This technique, involving tiny strands of cloth, is very challenging. I've never tried it.

The other Hawaiian technique, one I've used on small projects, is echo stitching. This is a quilting stitch that repeats the shape of the original design outward over the quilt like ripples on a pond. Of course, the more intricate the central design, the more complicated the echo stitching is going to be.

All these cultures and countless individuals made and continue to make their contributions to modern quilt making. Now techniques are evolving that incorporate new technologies. Computer programs can help you plan a quilt pattern or print a picture directly onto your fabric. The latest sewing machines add more choices to the way we embroider, appliqué, and quilt.

You can make a quilt without any thought of the quilters who came before, but imagining all those creative minds and clever hands working with you as you quilt can make you feel less alone. And remember, every single one of those quilters made a first quilt.

Faith and Color Choices

As we begin stitching all our pieces together in an art form that
has been influenced by so many different cultures, we need a
little faith that what we are making will work out, that it will be
okay. We can't know exactly what our quilt will look like until
it's together.

For example, Eden says even the colors surprised her when
she had her first quilt cover together. She had thought her quilt
was mostly red and blue and was surprised at all the yellow and
green. She put red vertical panels between her blocks and blue
horizontal panels between these rows. The effect actually star-
tled her every time she saw it for the first week or so. She wasn't
sure she liked it. Now she thinks the bold borders show strength
and go very well together.

Even though we can't know for sure how our color choices
will look once they are combined on the quilt top, quilters find
choosing the fabrics for their quilts their favorite part of quilt
making. Catherine Silhan says she loves "messing with colors."
The brighter, the better. Mary Ellen Giglio was conservative with
her fabrics for her first quilt and then she realized she could do
anything she wanted. Her second quilt uses much more vibrant
colors.

Colors spark emotional responses in us. Besides the learned
codes of color like red means stop and a blue line on a map is a
river, some colors like green calm us and others like red make
us more alert. Although much of what each of us considers
beautiful is subjective, there are certain color combinations that

scientists consider compatible. This compatibility relates to the colors' locations on the color wheel. Seeing colors together that harmonize affects us in much the same way music does.

Sometimes we like the effect so much, we overindulge. Marge Eaton told me she bought so much fabric over the years that when she first retired and felt she needed to save money, she was able to go a whole year without going to the fabric store. Meanwhile she was sewing more than ever.

Then there are all those optical illusions. Scientists speak of simultaneous contrast, which refers to a color-vision effect in which colors appear to change depending on the colors around them. The positioning of dark and light fabrics on a quilt top can make your quilt look three-dimensional. The only way we can anticipate these effects is to see our fabrics together as we collect them; even then we're often surprised.

Sharon Fields likes the Log Cabin pattern for this very reason. She does no planning and says she is often surprised at the shadows the color combinations create. Sometimes she can't believe the way they look. Those are her favorites. Eunice Borman can hardly wait to see how her quilt will go together. Nancy Collins likes to see if the colors she's chosen will go together the way she expects.

Not all surprises are pleasant, however. Joyce Swenson has a quilt top she put together that she feels didn't turn out. She made it because she wanted to try out a pattern and use up some scraps in the process. There are chunks of bright colors that make it look garish to her now. The cluttered effect of so many fabrics makes some people avoid scrap quilts entirely.

Not all our endeavors are going to suit us, although I suspect Joyce's quilt would suit someone else just fine. Her experience has shaken her faith in her ability, and now she finds choosing the fabrics the hardest part of quilting. We are probably our own harshest critics.

Faith and Piecing

Your next major decision will be whether to sew all your quilt patches together by machine or by hand. I think that nowadays people have less time for handwork and time, of course, will be a factor in the decision. Sister Betty Suther, who hand pieced her first quilt over a period of about a year, decided she wanted to make more quilts faster and moved to machine piecing. A lot of quilters who feel the same way avoid patterns with curves or other shapes that will require hand piecing.

I think both methods have their pleasures. Hand piecing is a bit more meditative. The pace is slower and more deliberate and perhaps a better stress reliever than machine piecing. I hold each piece of fabric in my hands longer and feel I have gained a more intimate knowledge of its texture and color. When the work is done, I feel a stronger attachment to the finished quilt because I spent more time inside it.

Hand piecing has the added advantage of being portable. A stack of pieces and a few tools can be carried to doctor's appointments or on vacation, making it possible to be creative during what would otherwise be wasted time.

On the other hand, it's fun to watch the pile of geometric pieces take shape in a quilt top. This happens much more quickly when you are machine piecing. In addition, there are several shortcuts I use to get the pieces together more quickly still. For example, I complete the first step on each of the blocks, press all the seams, and then move on to the second step. It has a little of the assembly-line feel, but it saves on sewing time that is often in short supply. The repetition of a particular step can become routine enough that there is room for reflection while I sew.

Chain piecing, in which a pair of pieces is fed under the sewing machine needle immediately after the previous pair, is another of those timesavers. The finished quilt is no less my own than it would be if I'd hand stitched every piece.

I like to have both types of projects, machine stitch and hand pieced, going at any given time. At this stage in the construction of a quilt, the two processes seem so completely different that they don't in any way interfere with each other. The machine-pieced project is going to be completed first, and there's always the danger I'll get bored with the hand-pieced one before it's finished. But that's all right, too. I can always come back to it later. As Marge Eaton says, it's almost like working on a new quilt to get one out that you've set aside for a while. Clearly I don't find it necessary to finish one quilt before I start the next, though I know some quilters do.

Whichever way of piecing you choose, you will be participating in a historic craft. The sewing machine as we know it was invented in 1846. Within a decade, it was in fairly common use, even among settlers on the plains. I've seen old photographs of families in front of sod houses that show a treadle sewing machine standing out in the yard. It's unlikely that they actually left the machine outside; they dragged it out for the photographer as a way of showing off a precious possession.

During the Civil War, when both cotton fabric and cotton thread became scarce, women on both sides of the conflict quit using their machines in favor of hand piecing because it used half as much thread. After the war they returned to their machines, even quilting on them with contrasting thread so it would be obvious that they were proud owners of sewing machines.

During the Great Depression, when saving was again a necessity, women returned to the scrap quilts and to hand piecing. As well as a way of using up every little bit of fabric, the quilts themselves fit well with the back-to-basics attitude of the time. Some women found it possible to sell their quilts during the Depression, which was a financial help to their families—a dynamic that demonstrates that more affluent people liked the notion of a homemade scrap quilt even if they didn't make it themselves.

Apparently, a lot of women who quilted during this era never got over the notion that the only way to make a quilt was by hand, and they may have passed that idea on to the next generation as well. They used their sewing machines for garment construction but not for their quilts. Marguerite Martin pieced all her thirty-plus quilts by hand. It gave her something to do while her husband watched TV in the evenings, she says.

With some faith, all those little pieces of fabric will fit together to make one quilt "like a puzzle," as Nancy Chaffee Parker says. You can't really know how all those colors and motifs are going to blend until it's done. And then they blend the way they do—maybe better than you expected, maybe not. But it's all one piece now instead of scores or hundreds. And even if it isn't exactly what you expected, it works. It takes faith to get this far.

Eden adds this about the bold borders she wasn't sure she liked: "Sleeping late one morning, I put the quilt over my head to block the sunshine. Stained glass! My clever quilt had found another way to be beautiful as the colors glowed and their [edges] blurred." What fun, to sleep with art!

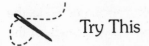 Try This

Next time you are sewing, whether you are feeding pieces under your sewing machine needle or wearing a thimble and stitching by hand, think of how the pieces of your life fit together, how the people in your life form your family and your community. Have you found your place in the scheme of things? Do you have enough faith to make the most of where you find yourself? Is there some aspect of your life you'd like to rip out? Would the rest hold together if you did? Is this unwanted piece something that can't be changed, and you need, instead, to learn to live with it better? Maybe you could cover this piece with some figurative spider-web embroidery . . .

chapter four

Great Deeds Wrought at Great Risks

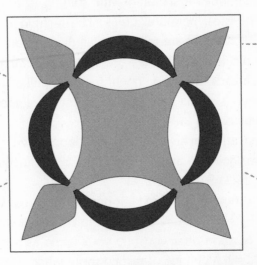

Appliqué

Appliqué is the process of sewing an intricately shaped piece on top of another fabric. Draw your shape on paper for a pattern and trace the shape onto the back of your fabric. Add one-fourth of an inch when you cut it out. Clip all inward curves with a cut almost to the stitching line. Clip all outward curves with a V. Press the seam allowance under all the way around. Using thread that matches the fabric, sew your piece in place with tiny overcast stitches that loop over the folded edge of the patch and into the base or lining fabric.

Right Effort

Traditional appliqué is one of the most exacting and time-con-suming techniques associated with quilting. It also produces some of the most beautiful quilts. The technique itself takes practice. Stitches that are too large will detract from the beauty of your quilt. If your stitches are too small, catching only a couple of threads, the fabric might fray and pull away from the stitches. There's a little more risk and a lot more effort involved in attempting one of these quilts.

My first attempt to make a hand-appliquéd quilt was a failure. I was going to make a red, white, and blue quilt to com-memorate the U.S. bicentennial.

I'm glad now that I didn't cut out all the pieces for the pro-ject when I started. You're supposed to cut out all the pieces of your quilt as soon after you buy your fabric as possible. That way there's still a chance of getting more fabric if you discover you don't have enough or if you make a mistake, as I did with the curtain panel. Instead, I cut out just enough for a block or two, which left most of the red, white, and blue fabrics intact for other projects, though after more than twenty-five years, I still have a little left.

The center of each block on the quilt I thought I was going to make was to be a white square with tiny hook-shaped blue and red pieces that fit together to outline a white star. I actually appliquéd two or three of these stars before I got too frustrated with the project and gave up. I think I may have gone ahead and pieced the stripes and squares around one of them and made that one block into a pillow. I don't remember. It wouldn't have lasted. I was trying so hard to hide my appliqué stitches that the pieces were pulling out before I even got through sewing them.

The experience kept me from trying hand appliqué again until fairly recently, when I made a few small projects. For a long time it didn't seem worth the effort, even after I learned what I had been doing wrong with that first abandoned project. The next quilt I made was machine appliquéd and did not involve nearly the same level of risk. I don't know if I'm more willing to risk failure now or more confident that I can find some way around any quilt-making problem. However, I'll be the first to admit that I still avoid certain types of projects because they look to me as though they'll take more effort than they're worth.

When I begin a quilt, I try to give some thought to what my efforts will yield. A quilt that stretches my skills will bless me with additional knowledge and a better appreciation of other quilters' efforts. I hope that what I learn about myself at the same time will carry over into other aspects of my life. If the quilt I am starting is intended for someone else, I hope that my efforts will bring that person pleasure.

Right effort is another of the Buddhist's eight steps toward happiness. But it isn't simply *effort* that is important. That would suggest that life is supposed to be a struggle. It is *right* effort that is the key. Our time, talents, and other resources must be directed toward the right thing. Our purpose for desiring to do this particular task relates directly to this right thing. But once we understand our purpose and begin, our effort in that direction must be right as well.

Of course, I tend to meditate on this kind of thing after I've already started the quilt. My efforts are too often needed elsewhere, and I don't want to listen to voices that remind me I need to clean the house, for example. I have discovered, however, that working on a quilt, whatever stage of construction it's in, for an hour or even half an hour in the evening relieves a great deal of stress. This allows me to sleep better at night and thus lets me better use my energies the following day.

My boss, Irene Brown, explains it by saying she can't wind down all at once. The handwork is permission to sit down and relax. Continuing to have her hands busy allows her to taper off from the tensions and rush of the day. This is just one more reason to believe quilting is the right thing for me to be doing most evenings. The task itself, as well as the finished project, is worth the effort.

On the other hand, there are occasions when our very best efforts, those that have the greatest impact, can seem almost effortless at the time. A few years ago, I made a baby blanket for a family that had just begun attending our church. When Sarah was born, I took the blanket along with a package of disposable diapers to the family's little house. I was shown into a crowded bedroom where the little girl slept and cheerfully compared the newborn face to baby pictures of the mother. The young woman was tired but pleased to show off her child and very happy to have her finally in her arms. She thanked me profusely for the gifts, and I left after staying only a few minutes.

I thought the diapers were probably the most useful gift I'd given. I saw the blanket a couple of times when her mother or grandmother brought Sarah to church, but otherwise I didn't think much about it. Because the mother had to work as many hours as possible at a department store, she wasn't in church often. When I'd see her at work, she would update me on her child's progress. And on one of these occasions, she reported that Sarah had outgrown the blanket and they had hung it on the wall of the girl's room.

That simple little blanket, which I'd made from leftovers, had been so appreciated it was now a wall hanging. Of all the things I have knit, crocheted, or sewn, I count that little blanket as one of my best efforts.

It didn't involve any risk for me, of course, except the possibility of its being rejected. How sad if this kind of fear has stopped someone from acting on a generous impulse. Fear that our efforts may not be good enough, may not measure up to someone else's standards, has stopped people from all kinds of things before they even got started. In those cases, they miss out on even more than the prospective recipient does.

Another time quilt making can take on a certain risk is when the quilter is a man. It's a little odd that this should be so, but quilting is so clearly considered a woman's craft that very few men even attempt it. I remember a little human-interest story in my local newspaper a few years back about a man who made quilts for his family. When there are dozens of women quilting in the same community, the fact that he rated an article indicates the perception that male quilters are unusual.

I talked to two male quilters for this book. Ken signed up for a quilting class with his wife and learned along with her. He was quick to tell me that he didn't stay with it, moving on instead to other hobbies, while his wife continues to quilt. He made four or five quilted projects that they still use around the house.

I think I was expecting to find that men would enjoy quilting for different reasons than women, but Ken's favorite part was the same as many women's: He liked mixing and matching the colors.

Danny McReynolds enjoys showing off his quilting projects. In fact, he's shown his quilts at the county fair, where he's won a blue ribbon, which is how I learned that he was quilting.

His quilt making began as a way to use up the fabric left from his wife's and daughters' sewing projects. He had done some other fabric crafts before he decided to quilt. Like so many of us, he plunged in first and then bought books on the subject. His favorite part is piecing. He likes watching his plan come together. He makes the tops and layers them, but his mother-in-law does the hand quilting for him. He's tried to learn from her, but his "fingers don't want to work that way," he says. He's tied a few quilts and is tempted to get a quilting machine.

It's probably true that strides in feminism have opened the door for men to cross the gender lines as well and there are more men willing to try quilting now than there would have been fifty or even thirty years ago. However, I have heard a few women mention how their husbands would help them piece their quilts. One laughed about how quickly he could get rid of the sewing if someone came to the door.

A little embarrassment or the possibility of rejection is insignificant when you think of what some people have risked for what they believed was right. Believe it or not, quilts have played a role in many political and social risks or efforts in America.

Great Risks

There is a quilt pattern called the Underground Railroad. Until shortly after the Civil War, the pattern of 4-Patch squares and triangles, which form a diagonal "road" across the quilt top, was called Jacob's Ladder. It is believed by some that quilts of this pattern were used to relay coded messages on the Underground Railroad.

For many years before the Civil War, a network of brave abolitionists helped escaping slaves on their flight to Canada and freedom. This network was called the Underground Railroad, though it was neither a railroad nor a series of underground tunnels. "Railroad" was taken as a metaphor for the effort because railroads were relatively new and fascinating at the time. The use of the word *underground* to refer to secret activities dates back to the 1570s during the Christian Reformation. This Underground Railroad was, of necessity, a secret operation.

If you helped runaway slaves in any way, whether providing food and shelter or clothes to help them blend in with the free population, let alone actually moving them from one safe house or station to the next, you were breaking the law. Your nearest neighbor might not feel the same way about emancipation without proclamation as you did; he might think your efforts were not only wrong-headed but also dangerous to the community. Your neighbor might feel a responsibility to turn you in.

The signals used in carrying out these illegal, but moral, efforts were by definition covert and therefore unknown to the average person. There is little documentation of exactly how the Underground Railroad functioned. There are a few published accounts, but most people, even after the war, were afraid of reprisals and continued to conceal the details.

It is unlikely that secret maps were hidden in the Underground Railroad quilts as some suppose. No matter how much help you might have, it would be difficult to finish a quilt with a hidden map before the information became obsolete. In fact, it's much more likely that the Underground Railroad quilt pattern became popular after the war to commemorate the efforts of the brave "conductors," "stationmasters," and "engineers." The Jacob's Ladder pattern may have been renamed Underground Railroad because the song "Jacob's Ladder" was one of several spirituals believed to contain coded signals in the verses.

The Log Cabin quilt is also rumored to have been used as a signal. The center of each Log Cabin block is a small square, which is traditionally red. If the center was black, or so tradition goes, it marked a safe house on the Underground Railroad. This is possible but also unlikely. The Log Cabin quilt, like the

Underground Railroad quilt, did not become popular until after the Civil War. The Log Cabin quilt commemorated Abraham Lincoln, the slain "log cabin president." As such, it was a political statement, at least, if not a signal on the Underground Railroad. Making either one of these quilts during the years following the Civil War may have helped Northern women grieve, not only for President Lincoln, but for their own lost loved ones as well.

Quilts, as well as other everyday things, may have been used to identify safe houses along the Underground Railroad, however. It is believed that quilts were used in this way during the Revolutionary War, as well. The color of the quilt hung on a clothesline and whether the face side or the backing was visible from the road indicated whether it was safe to come in with information for the patriots or to bring in a spy who needed to be hidden. During both wars, next-door neighbors, and even family members, were often on opposite sides of the conflict. Signals were probably agreed on and changed regularly to avert suspicion.

Quilts may have been used on the plantations as signals to slaves waiting for a chance to escape. The household quilts were aired regularly, and the masters might not have paid too much attention to the routine as long as it was being done. This inattention would have given the house slaves, who would have had the best knowledge of the master's movements, the opportunity to signal when it was time to run. Whether the code used particular quilt patterns, such as the Wagon Wheel to indicate that it was time to load the wagon for escape that night, or whether the signals were prearranged by those involved and varied from plantation to plantation is unknown. I think the latter is more likely.

Although there seems to be no firsthand, documented evidence that quilts were used as signals, the notion is so much a part of quilting tradition that I wouldn't discount it. But whether quilts were used as signals or not, a few almost surely traveled the Underground Railroad. The poor refugees of the South could not have been equipped for the colder weather of the North. Blankets were almost certainly donated along with clothes and food.

Twenty years or so before the Civil War actually started, abolitionists were holding handicraft fairs, which included quilts, to raise money for their anti-slavery campaigns and to keep their message in front of their communities.

During the Civil War, women on both sides of the conflict made quilts, which they raffled off to raise money for care packages for soldiers or to donate to widows' and veterans' relief funds and other causes associated with the war. Some people, probably men mostly, objected to women's involvement in any kind of enterprise that involved money. By taking part in these activities, some patriotic women probably risked the wrath of their husbands and fathers.

In the North, the Sanitary Commission enlisted the help of women in forming Soldier Relief Circles to sew and knit clothing and bandages. Women were asked to pledge three hours a week. The Sanitary Commission requested quilts that were 7 feet long and 50 inches wide. More than 250,000 quilts were sent to Union soldiers during the war. Few of these quilts survive, however, since they must have seen some hard service. Those quilts that made it home with the soldiers would have been put into everyday use.

The goal of the quilters would have been quantity rather than quality, anyway. The quilts were probably done in simple patterns such as 4-Patch or 9-Patch without too much worry over any blocks that were pieced from mismatched scraps.

To the quilter, these quilts would hardly have been considered difficult to make, but to the soldiers, who were always short on supplies and yearning for a touch of home, the quilts must have been priceless. They represented, in the very deepest sense, the women's best efforts. They represented their prayers in action.

In the South, women raffled off Gunboat quilts. The funds went to build up the South's navy. Three gunboats were financed through the women's efforts. After a year or so of war and several naval defeats, the women's enthusiasm for the cause waned. They turned their efforts to the soldiers instead and raised money for medical supplies.

After another year or so of the North's blockades, cotton was so scarce it was nearly impossible to find. Women still managed to make quilts for their soldiers. Old clothes, draperies, and even carpets were cut up for blankets.

Kinder, Gentler Risk

In *Quilts from the Civil War* (Lafayette, Calif.: C & T Publishing, Inc, 1997), author Barbara Brackman relates a romance that grew as a result of one of the Sanitary Commission quilts and a note a sixteen-year-old quilter attached to it.

Fannie Chester listed the names of all the women who had worked on the quilt along with her own address. The quilt ended up in the possession of Capt. Robert Emmett Fisk. Robert, glad not only for the quilt but for a chance to write to a young woman, penned a thank-you note to Fannie. At the end of the letter, he invited her to write again so he would know his letter had reached her.

Fannie decided she had overstepped the rules of propriety by seeking a letter from a strange man and asked her older sister Elizabeth to write to him and explain. Robert was eleven years Fannie's senior.

Elizabeth took up the task, writing that Fannie was busy with school duties. Robert wrote again, asking *her* to continue the correspondence. Elizabeth had misgivings but justified her bold behavior by writing that civilians were urged to write to friends in the army.

After the war ended, Robert visited Elizabeth and they were married, happily ever after, or so we suppose. One never knows what relationships might develop out of an act of sacrifice.

Little Acts of Defiance

While women were happy to give their quilts away for relief of the soldiers that they looked on as their own sons and brothers, they were not willing to see them taken by the enemy. There are numerous stories of quilts being hidden, usually buried, with other valuables such as the family's silver, where they could protect it from nicks. In fact, one of the quilters who contacted me said her grandmother remembers being told just this kind of family story by her mother and grandmother.

Most of these stories come out of the Southern states because these residents suffered the most from marauding soldiers. This was especially true of those in the path of General Sherman's army on its march from Atlanta, Georgia, to the sea. The troops were instructed to "forage liberally on the country." These soldiers took horses and mules, food and bedding. Also, to the quilter, the very idea of a quilt made with her own hands going to comfort the enemy was at least as abhorrent as the loss of the quilt itself.

Fannie Kreeger Haller was ten years old when she saw one of her mother's appliquéd quilts taken by Union soldiers. Her family lived in one of the counties of Missouri that bordered Kansas. The U.S. Army, which had occupied Missouri since the war began, had just issued Military Order No. 11. This order directed that certain counties be evacuated.

The order was a response to Confederate sympathizer William Quantrill and his gang's raid on "Free State" Lawrence, Kansas, in August 1863. Quantrill and his men, as well as other groups of Rebel Raiders, were known to be getting aid and comfort from area residents. Missourians with certificates of loyalty to the Union were allowed to move to designated military outposts or to Kansas. Everyone else was simply ordered to leave in a matter of days.

We don't have the whole story, so we don't know if the Kreegers were slow to move or if the quilt was stolen by a soldier sent to spread the word of the order. Young Fannie might not have understood what was happening at the time, but she knew that the military order entered into her family's plight. The law still rankled when Fannie reproduced the quilt from memory many years later. Though her mother's quilt would probably have been called a Hickory Leaf, Fannie named hers Order No. 11, and it was published as such in the *Kansas City Star* in 1929. A block made from that pattern is illustrated at the beginning of this chapter.

When Fannie designed her quilt from memory, she may have been thinking less of political issues than she was of her mother. I'm sure Fannie saw both her quilt and the name she gave it as tributes to the woman who saw her own handiwork stolen.

Quilts made during this period often announced the politics of the quilter. Some Civil War–era quilts feature slogans like "Union Forever." These quilts might have been a little dangerous to display, depending on where you lived.

Palmyra Mitchell, another Missourian, was married to a Kentuckian with strong Southern sympathies. One day during the Civil War, a troop of Union soldiers rode up to the farm and demanded to see the Union flag. On hearing that the Mitchells didn't have one, the soldiers said they'd better find one. The soldiers promised to return, and, if they didn't see a flag, they'd burn the house.

Palmyra found scraps enough in her stash to piece together a small flag. She added two loops to hang it vertically, but she put those loops on the side with the stripes and no stars. The flag would have hung upside down. The soldiers didn't notice or didn't care and spared the house, but it was a risky act of defiance. I'm sure as Palmyra pieced her flag, she was hoping that her efforts would save her home. At the same time, she needed to stay true to her own convictions in this one small way. The fragile old flag is now displayed at Missouri's Weston Historical Museum.

The *arpilleristas* of Chile are a more recent example of risks involving quilts. During General Pinochet's regime, which lasted from 1973 to 1990, basic freedoms were restricted and opponents were imprisoned. Peasant women got together and sewed *arpilleras*, which translates as sackcloths. These small quilts quite literally told their stories of death and torture. The women wrote their stories and sewed them into pockets in the back of their quilts.

The process served as therapy for these mothers and wives of "the disappeared," but it also formed an organized protest. The *arpilleras* were smuggled into the churches and from there out of the country. Sales of the quilts raised needed money for the women, but more important, their quilts helped draw attention to the human rights violations in their country. Who knows how much of an effect these stories had on the eventual pressure that made Pinochet step down.

Of a somewhat different nature are the quilts made by refugees in Quetta, Pakistan, 150 miles from the former Taliban stronghold of Kandahar, Afghanistan. When thousands more refugees crowded into Quetta as a result of the coalition forces' military campaign in Afghanistan, Church World Services launched a quilt-making project to provide blankets to newly arriving refugees and offer some income to the women who made them. Monetary gifts from Christians all over the world to One Great Hour of Sharing allowed Church World Services to buy fabric in Pakistan and then train and pay the 400 women they employed to make the quilts. Twenty-five thousand quilts were made and distributed within three months. A second quilt-making project has since begun in Kabul, Afghanistan.

Think of what this program means to the quilt makers. They are earning money for their families, but even more, they are helping others in their country.

Sometimes it's not so much the quilt that makes a state-ment, as what is done with it. Quilting clubs often make baby quilts for hospitals or lap-robe–size quilts for nursing homes. Some donate quilts to homeless shelters or to sheriff's depart-ments for accident or fire victims. Quilts collected and sent to the children of Afghanistan or other war-torn countries make an even stronger statement.

The organizational nature of these projects minimizes the risk for the quilter. Imagine walking up to a homeless person and handing over a quilt. Would you feel some risk? What if this person acts strangely? What if witnesses think you're stupid? What if he or she resents the charity? What if it's the only act of kindness he or she has experienced in recent memory? And what difference might it make?

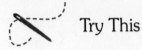 Try This

Put your best effort into a quilt for someone society considers an outcast. Perhaps you can make a baby quilt and donate it to a shelter or hospital. Can you get a quilt to a victim of domestic violence or a teenage mother? Check for current programs through religious or service organizations.

Perhaps you'd like to make this quilt entirely out of scraps. You can even piece together leftover batting by overlapping the pieces and trimming through both layers. The pieces will fit together exactly, and you can loosely whipstitch them together. Use up some larger odds and ends for the backing. Meditate on your efforts and try to live your Zen.

chapter five

The Words of My Mouth

Zen Quilt

Sampler

Sandra Paulsen Detrixhe

Concordia, Kansas

2002 - 200

Mark for Quilting

When the quilt cover is pieced together, it's time to mark it for the quilting stitches. A hard lead pencil is the cheapest instrument for this task, but special pencils are available. You can buy stencils, copy patterns, or make up your own. You won't need to mark your quilt if you simply follow the seams of your piecing, perhaps ¼-inch inside each seam. An alternative to quilting, tying your quilt, won't require any marking either. But if you're feeling creative and brave and want to cover your quilt with swirls or leaves or diagonal lines, mark these lines on your quilt cover to follow when you quilt.

And the Meditation of My Heart

I had run away for an afternoon "fling." My husband was attending the Kansas Farm Bureau Convention, and I had the day off work. I drove to Salina, a city about fifty miles away and the site of the nearest Hobby Lobby. I had three plastic bags of swatches and was having a good time among the bolts of fabric. A woman I'd guess to be in her late sixties was roaming the aisles, too, and we would meet up now and again. I guess my swatches gave me away because she pegged me as a quilter very quickly.

In the juvenile print section she told me about the quilt she was making for a grandchild and asked my opinion of a bunny print. "Neither of my daughters-in-law sew," she said, wrinkling her nose. "They say they don't have time. Well, one of them doesn't, but the other one—" She shook her head.

"We can usually make the time to do the things we really want to. Sewing just may not be one of those things for either of them," I said.

"They just don't know what's important," she countered.

I let it go, but I can't imagine that her attitude is going to lead either of her daughters-in-law to sewing. It seems to me that if these young women don't sew, the quilts the mother-in-law makes could be that much more appreciated. I say *could be* because it's going to depend a lot on the voice she uses when she gives them.

Marguerite Martin's story of making the Lone Star quilt as a teenager was given to me by her daughter-in-law, Kathy Martin.

Kathy interviewed the quilter on audiocassette for me. The tape clearly reveals the women's mutual affection and Kathy's respect for the quilts the older woman has made.

The speech of these two women and the woman at Hobby Lobby tell us a great deal about them. This is why right speech is another of the keys to happiness. Imagine how much trouble we could avoid if we were always clever enough to say the right thing at the right time, or smart enough to know when to say nothing at all.

Our quilts can speak for us sometimes. I have on hand a couple of baby quilts. The first I made intentionally to save for my first grandchild. It is a 9-Patch with a cartoon-farm-animal print. It seemed appropriate for farmer grandparents to give a city baby. The second quilt was an excuse to try a new technique.

I have no immediate hope of grandchildren. I don't want my children to have children until it's right for them. I certainly don't want them to feel pressured to have children. But on a purely personal, selfish level, I'd love to have a grandchild. Making baby quilts is a way for me to express that desire. And if the time comes when I have to accept that none of my children want to have babies, I don't think I'll have any trouble finding someone else who'll want the quilts.

As my dad liked to say, one of the easiest things in the world to "adopt" is a grandchild. As families become more scattered, young people have babies far from the support of real grandparents. A little extra interest and attention from pretend grandparents can be helpful.

So, I make my baby quilts and try not to mention grandchildren to my children. I trust them to know what's important and appropriate for them.

Quilts as Historical Records

I'm not the first to speak through a quilt, of course. Women have always done it. Perhaps especially before women could vote, but even after the Nineteenth Amendment in 1920 women used quilts to announce their politics. As we saw in the previous chapter, sometimes they took some risks to "speak" their minds.

Politics in quilts is obvious in the names of early quilt blocks, if not in the appearance of the quilt itself. Order No. 11 from the last chapter is one example as is Fifty-four forty or fight, a slogan from the 1830s and 1840s. This slogan refers to the border between the United States and Great Britain in the Oregon Territory. The area between latitude 42° North and 54° 40' was occupied by both countries since the signing of an 1818 treaty. The compromise in 1846 was 49°, but the slogan lives on in a star and 4-Patch block.

There are quilts that announce the quilter's political leanings. Everyone knows Democrat donkeys and Republican elephants. There's a Liberty Star and a Union Star that probably go back to the Civil War, along with Yankee Pride, Yankee Puzzle, and Lincoln's Platform. Whig Rose has to be even older since the party began to splinter with the defeat of their candidate in 1852 and dissolved entirely in 1860. Whether the quilt block, Whig's Defeat, was made in sorrow or joy, is now impossible to know.

There are quilts named after political leaders and their wives such as Washington's Puzzle and Martha Washington's Wreath, Madison Patch and Dolly Madison's Star, Jackson Star (after Andrew rather than Michael) and Harrison Rose (named for William Henry Harrison, not Harrison Ford). Old Tippecanoe, a 16-Patch of split squares that has been done in several different arrangements, also refers to William Henry Harrison, ninth president of the United States. He got the nickname after defeating the Shawnee Indians in the Battle of Tippecanoe in 1811.

Several other quilt blocks were named to commemorate events that are now familiar only to historians. Collectors preserved the titles and the appearances of the blocks. Key among these collectors was Carrie Alma Hackett Hall. When Mrs. Hall decided she had made more quilts than her family would ever use, she began collecting blocks and researching their history. Her book, *The Romance of the Patchwork Quilt in America,* written with Rose G. Kretsinger (New York: Bonaza Book, 1935), discusses the origin of the patterns in her collection, which numbered more than one thousand.

Hall donated the blocks to the Thayer Museum at the University of Kansas in 1938. Her 1935 book contains only black-and-white pictures, but 800 of those blocks are pictured in full color in *Carrie Hall Blocks* by Bettina Havig (Paducah, KY: American Quilter's Society, 1999).

One of the blocks in this collection is called Burgoyne Surrounded. Burgoyne was a British general during the Revolutionary War. In an effort to invade New York State from Canada, he found himself surrounded by a much larger American army and surrendered at Saratoga, New York. The battle helped bring France into the war and is considered one of the more decisive battles in history. The event is commemorated forever in very elaborate blocks made up of rather tiny squares arranged in a circle around a pattern of larger squares.

Nelson's Victory, a 16-Patch with the center squares done in a pinwheel design, refers to Horatio Nelson's victory at Trafalgar. Considered Great Britain's greatest admiral, Nelson defeated the combined French and Spanish fleets in 1805 and established Britain as a naval power. The development of this block some thirty years after the American Revolution made a statement about the United States' changing relationship with England.

The Lemon Star is made of eight equal diamond shapes and is the most basic star pattern. It is the foundation for many other star patterns, most lilies, and the center of the Lone Star and other expanding star patterns. The name is a misspelling and mispronunciation of LeMoyne. The LeMoyne brothers, Pierre and Jean Baptiste, were early settlers to France's colony of Louisiana. Pierre founded what is now Ocean Springs, Mississippi, and was the first governor of the colony. Jean Baptiste founded New Orleans in 1718 while he was governor. The quilt pattern honors both brothers and probably didn't travel far from the region until after the Louisiana Purchase in 1803. If it did, it's possible that the fact that the LeMoyne brothers expanded France's territory into what England considered hers was the reason for the name change. I think it's more likely, however, that New England quilters only learned of the pattern nearly a hundred years after the LeMoynes started their settlements. French names and the history of Louisiana were both unfamiliar and the name was simply corrupted to Lemon.

Kansas Troubles has a combination pinwheel and saw-toothed or feathered look. It refers to the war over whether Kansas would be a slave state or a free state, which began well before and contributed to the beginning of the Civil War.

One of the men who had a hand in the passage of the Compromise of 1850 and the Kansas–Nebraska Act, both of which added fuel to the fire along the Kansas–Missouri border, was Sen. Stephen A. Douglas. He is best known for his debates with Abraham Lincoln when they ran against each other, first for the Senate in 1858 (Douglas won) and for president in 1860. Although Douglas lost the latter race, he does have a quilt block named for him, Little Giant, a nickname he got because of his small stature and political fearlessness.

Coxey's Camp is a small 4-Patch inside a square surrounded by another square. The corners of each block are squares, which combine with the corners of adjacent blocks to form larger squares. The effect is to make the center 4-Patch of each block look rather lonely. It is a reference to Jacob Coxey who, in the depression of the 1890s, formed an "army" of unemployed men to march into Washington, D.C. He left Massillon, Ohio, with one hundred men, expecting his ranks to swell to one hundred thousand on the way. In May 1894, fewer than four hundred followed him into Washington where he was arrested for walking on the Capitol lawn. I can't be sure if the quilt block honored Coxey's cause or ridiculed his defeat.

Between 1930 and 1932, during the Great Depression, Mrs. Fannie B. Shaw made a quilt called "Prosperity Is Just Around the Corner." In thirty separate panels, she makes fun of the political slogan by depicting people of many different professions looking around a red brick wall, waiting for prosperity. Even an elephant and a donkey are watching. The center block is a farmer, her husband presumably, plowing a field with no time to wait and watch. Uncle Sam arrives in the final block with relief money rather than prosperity. The quilt belongs to the Dallas Museum of Art and is pictured in the *Twentieth Century's Best American Quilts* (Golden, CO: Primedia Special Interest Publications, 1999).

More recently, I can cite the ever-growing AIDS Quilt as one that makes a powerful political and social statement. Quilters continue to express their feelings of world events, and quilts that commemorate the destruction of the World Trade Center towers have been featured in quilting magazines in the past several months. If you have been anywhere near a fabric store or the fabric section of a department store, you have noticed the increased number of fabrics with patriotic themes. Quilting in the wake of tragedy is still a way of facing grief and finding comfort for many people.

Quilts as Personal Records

Besides speaking for us in a political sense, quilts speak to us on a more personal level. Many people have told me about treasuring a quilt because they recognize some of the pieces as leftovers from their clothes or those of relatives. "Many grandchildren have been talked to sleep," Becky Fooshee Walters of Burns, Kansas, writes, "as stories were told regarding different pieces of fabric that made up Grandma's quilt blocks." Store-bought quilts don't come with stories, she notes.

Pauline Palmer Meek shared a very touching story of memories in the fabric of a quilt. All through her grade-school days in the little town of Miltonvale, Kansas, Pauline had two special friends: Geneva, who was also her second cousin, and Esther, who lived across the street. From mud pies and swimming to competing scholastically and making music together in high school, they were always fast friends. On December 7, 1933, Geneva woke early, complaining of a terrible headache. By afternoon, she was dead of spinal meningitis.

About a year later, Geneva's mother asked Esther and Pauline for scraps of material left from their school dresses, particularly from the sewing class they had taken together as freshmen. From these scraps Geneva's mother made three quilts, souvenirs of the girls' friendship, and gave one to Esther and one to Pauline.

It's been nearly seventy years since Geneva's sudden death. Pauline and Esther still write each other and miss Geneva. She says if she still had the quilt she'd be able to identify which fabrics were hers and some of the others as well. The quilt was used to keep her children snug and warm in the cold bedrooms of her old farmhouse. "The love it represented had a special warmth," Pauline writes.

Imagine the courage of the grieving mother to face the loss of her daughter this way. But imagine, too, how much healing took place as she pieced and quilted and remembered.

Nancy Chaffee Parker told me about a memory quilt she made. Her family has a white wicker bassinet, which has been the first bed for three generations of babies. She remembers when she was a girl, it resided in her grandmother's laundry room when it wasn't needed. Nancy would tuck her dolls to sleep in it, knowing that she had slept in it and so had her father.

When she and her brother began their own families, asking to borrow the bassinet became the way of announcing a pregnancy. Her brother teased that he and Nancy had to stagger the arrival of their children so they wouldn't both need the bassinet at the same time.

The bassinet is now in the guest room at Nancy's parents' house. It awaits the next generation. Nancy's brother repainted it, and Nancy made a quilt for it. The quilt records the names and birthdates of all the babies who spent their first few months in the bassinet. "There's room to add more names," she adds.

New technology lets us put our memories on quilts in a way never imagined by earlier quilters. Pictures can be scanned into a computer, enlarged, and printed onto transfer paper, and then ironed onto cloth. Jean Gordon Wilcox, an employee at Country Cousins, the little fabric store near where I work, made a memory quilt for her father. She combined actual transferred photographs with appliquéd houses based on photographs and a few standard pieced quilt blocks.

When her father, eighty-five, turned his old photographs over to her, the experience of looking through the pictures brought back memories. It also prompted questions about her own early childhood and his life before she was born. One envelope of pictures was labeled "the little white house," the first place he and Jean's mother had lived together. The little house and the pleasure her parents took in it prompted Jean to make the memory quilt.

The center of the memory quilt is a 20-inch square depicting the farm with all the buildings appliquéd onto it. The older photographs were all black and white, naturally, and Jean had to rely on her own memory or her father's for the colors. When she asked her father what color the shutters had been, she discovered he had salvaged one before the house was torn down and had kept it in his garage. She got a chance to match her fabric to the green paint still visible on the old shutter. She also got another strong hint of what that house meant to her father.

The center block is surrounded by 10-inch blocks of appliquéd houses based on the photographs, actual photos of family members and of her father's dogs, and an embroidered map of the county marking the location of the little white house and of the town where he now lives. Jean reserved a block for a picture of him at eighty-four with a twenty-five-pound catfish he had just caught. She pieced Kansas Troubles and Kansas Sunflower blocks as well as one of her own design, Kansas Memories, which features a pieced windmill flanked by a sunflower and growing wheat.

"When I gave it at Christmas," she writes, "it sparked a day of reminiscing." It is now hanging on his living room wall where he can show if off to everyone. He has even set up a spotlight to shine on it. Jean's quilt speaks clearly of her love for her father, and that, I suspect, is part of what he's so pleased to show off.

Marsha Wentz made a memory quilt for her parents' fiftieth anniversary. This was eighteen years ago and the process was new. All the transfers were black and white, but that didn't matter. That quilt, too, stirred lots of memories.

Sharon Fields and Bonnie both told me that the memory quilts are their favorite ones to make. Sharon put pictures of all her grandchildren on a quilt and invited each one to write a message to their grandfather; then she gave the quilt to her husband. She made a quilt for a granddaughter's high school graduation and had the family sign it. She also made a handprint quilt for her mother-in-law.

Bonnie made a quilt for her son's high school graduation with all the photographs and newspaper articles from his years in high school sports. He didn't say much about it when she gave it to him, but the next day he had it spread out on the floor so he could read the articles. She told him she intended for him to take it to college with him, but he said no. He didn't want to do that. He didn't want anything to happen to that quilt.

Bonnie also made memory quilts for anniversaries and one for her husband with all his hunting pictures. She says she loves making them as gifts but needs to feel a real connection to the person she's sewing for. Other people have seen her quilts and asked her to make one for them, but she has declined, pleading lack of time. She doesn't want to do it except out of love.

Teresa LaFlair recently surprised her husband with a picture quilt. Like most husbands, he never ventures into his wife's sewing room so he had no idea what she was working on. The photographs all followed a hunting-and-fishing theme and featured him with his father and several of his friends. One of the friends, and his father, had both died a short time before, making those pictures particularly precious. Several of the other friends signed the quilt and wrote personal messages.

All of these quilts may have been made for a particular person, but they'll be treasured for their history by the next generation as well.

Records on Quilts

In a sense, the story behind a quilt is its soul. Whether it was made simply to keep a family member warm or to test a new pattern or to celebrate a life, there's a story woven into the fabric and stitches. Becky Fooshee Walters notes, "When I see old quilts in antique stores or at auctions, I wonder if there was no one left to want those works of art." Was there family left who cared less about the stories than about the money the quilts might bring? Becky adds, "I can't imagine my quilts being hauled away by strangers for any monetary sum. They are a part of where I came from."

We sometimes think of history as something from the distant past. But what we do today eventually becomes part of history. Too often, quilters failed to recognize their quilts as heirlooms and make no provision for their distribution. When this happens, the quilts themselves may be preserved, but the stories are lost. The voice of the quilter is silenced.

The saddest story I've heard regarding the fate of some old quilts involves two sisters, several years apart in age. The older sister had several quilts their mother had made in the 1920s. The younger may have had some, as well; I don't know.

The older sister died in her eighties, and a few years later her husband decided to move into a rest home. Since the couple had no children, his sister came to arrange an auction of everything he wasn't moving with him. Either she didn't know or didn't care what those quilts would have meant to the quilter's other daughter. They went up for sale along with all the rest of the items.

Because the couple were elderly and had lived in the same place for many years, there were many other antiques on the bill. The sale was well attended by antique dealers. The quilter's daughter tried to bid on the quilts but dropped out when the price went up to $400 and more. She had to watch her mother's quilts go off with strangers; quilts she felt should have been hers.

We can all understand how they legally belonged to the quilter's son-in-law, how he had every right to sell them. But we can also understand the younger daughter's desire to keep the quilts and their stories in the family. The older daughter may have wanted her to have them, too, But she never put it in writing—and now the quilts are gone.

A side note that probably increased the younger daughter's bitterness is the fact that the purpose of the sale, besides the need to take care of the no longer used items, was to raise money for the rest home. The old man died almost immediately upon moving in. His younger sister inherited the proceeds from the sale, including the sale of the quilts.

Joyce Swenson has decided that each of her nieces and nephews will get one of her quilts. She had always wished someone would give her a quilt and then she finally decided to make her own. She's hoping that her nieces and nephews will all use their quilts and remember family. Her own children, she adds, have about as many quilts as they want.

Florence Baker has written down a very similar bequest. Each family member can take one of her quilts. Florence's mother made most of them, although Florence and her sister made a few. Florence has no offspring and her twin sister is deceased so the invitation extends to cousins. "They all get along pretty well," she says.

Of course, even if the quilt stays in the family, some of the story can get lost anyway. We shouldn't take for granted that our children will know which grandmother made those old quilts in the trunk. Write down everything you can find out about the quilter and her quilt. Put the story with the quilt or with other important documents. If the story is going to be stored with the quilt, make sure it's on acid-free paper or it will eventually stain the fabric.

A lot of quilters sign their quilts. This has been done for a long time and is occasionally a clue to the history of an antique quilt whose story has slipped away. Names were embroidered on at first. In the mid-1800s, indelible ink was invented and quilters began autographing their quilts in ink. The trend is back to embroidery now, I think. Some genealogically minded quilters use their maiden name as well when they sign their quilts. Dates are important, too, of course.

Occasionally a quilt lends itself to an entire history embroidered on a block. A sample of a record block is illustrated at the beginning of this chapter. I worked up blocks as models for the artists to follow when they drew the illustrations used at the beginning of the chapters of this book. Two of those blocks were made to be part of another quilt I'm working on. I decided the rest, along with a few other blocks, will go together to make a twin-size quilt once the artists are through with them.

I imagine I will refer to the quilt as the Zen quilt because of this book, but it is really a Sampler quilt since every block will be different. I don't generally use my maiden name, but I included it on the record block because it is part of my historical identity. The town and state place the quilt geographically.

Since I had also made a couple of blocks for the illustrators of *The Everything® Quilting Book* I decided those blocks would go into the quilt, as well. That put the beginning date in 2002. I'm not sure when I'll actually finish the quilt. While it's more difficult to embroider the information on after the quilt is all put together, it isn't impossible. I'll add the last digit for the completion date when the rest of it is done. I'm counting on finishing it before 2010!

Records of Quilts

The daughter of an avid quilter expressed a common regret of quilters and their offspring when she said she wishes she had kept a record of all the quilts her mother has made. At ninety-five, her mother's still quilting. Marguerite Martin and others told me they couldn't remember how many quilts they had made.

Since I doubt if my memory is going to be any better than theirs, I recently started a quilt diary. I wish I had started it sooner, and I wish I had taken more pictures of my babies with the quilts I made for them. Late is better than never, though. I've photographed the quilts I still have, including the ones

Grandma Benson made. I searched through our family photographs and found a few with a quilt in them. Now I try to take a picture of each of my quilts at some point in the construction as well as one when it is finished. On a page opposite these pictures, I record the name I use to refer to the quilt, the pattern name, the dates (as near as I can remember since I'm working backward on some of these quilts), and anything else I remember about the quilt and its construction.

For example, the Charm quilt is from a Double Axe Head pattern. It was pieced and quilted entirely by hand and was the first quilt I put in my freestanding, rotating hoop. A large portion of the Cathedral Window quilt was pieced in the car on the way to Kansas City and the University of Kansas Medical Center when our youngest child was undergoing treatments there. These are part of the stories of these quilts.

The few quilts that I have that I didn't make will get their pages in the book as well. When I give away my baby quilts or any of the others, I plan to photocopy the pages from my diary and present them along with the quilt. My hope is that the diary—besides being a scrapbook for me—will preserve the stories of the quilts, even the ones that get used and eventually thrown away.

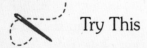 Try This

Make a memory quilt, either with transferred photographs or appliqués based on pictures. You can make this for yourself or for a loved one. Consider including blocks to represent occupations, hobbies, and major events. Sketch out some original blocks, but also look at the names of old standards. As you sew, consider what each block has to say to you.

If you're not ready to make a full-size quilt, consider making a pillow. You could make four small blocks for each side. You could divide the blocks between your personal side and your business side, or your private side and public side, or any other arrangement that makes sense to you.

Join the Sisterhood

Backing and Batting

While cotton batting sounds authentic, polyester is more widely available and will give you the lightest-weight, fluffiest, snuggliest last-forever quilt. Spread it out a day or so before you need it, spritz the wrinkles with water and pat them as flat as possible, and then leave it to dry.

Extra-wide fabric will let you avoid a seam in your backing, but if you want a prettier back you will need to piece two lengths of fabric. If you split one length and sew the two halves on either side of the second length, your seams will be near the edges of the bed instead of down the middle and less likely to show.

The Retreat

How we act, what we do matters. This is, of course, obvious to everyone. Most of us are taught honesty and fairness and lament the fate of those who are not. Most of the time we don't need to wonder how we should conduct ourselves. Stress, fatigue, and momentary bursts of selfishness might cause us to behave badly, but we become aware of it and regret our lapses.

Because how we act is the gauge those around us use in determining who we are, right conduct is one of the Buddhist keys to happiness. This doesn't surprise us. A dilemma about what we should do will bring us to prayer or meditation about as fast as anything.

It was Friday, January 10, and it was cold. I worked late and drove directly from the office to the Manna House, just a few blocks away. The Manna House is a spiritual center operated by the Sisters of St. Joseph of Concordia, Kansas. It occupies an old brick building, which was, until around 1950, a Catholic hospital. It has been the Manna House of Prayer since 1978, offering a wide range of spiritual workshops and retreats.

The evening before, I had loaded a basket with the Take Along blocks I was quilting and the few supplies I would need for the weekend into my Mustang. A Take Along quilt is one in which each block is layered with the batting and backing and quilted individually, then sewn together later. This makes it possible to take your quilt along with you on vacation and to doctor's appointments and so forth. I had chosen the Dresden Plate design because the quilting stitches follow the lines of the appliqué and are complete within each block, thus making it possible to sew the blocks together after the quilting is done without worrying about breaks in a quilting pattern. A Dresden Plate is illustrated at the beginning of this chapter.

I had two blocks ready to appliqué and two more that were ready to quilt. I was going to attend my first quilter's retreat. Sister Betty Suther leads two a year. The one I was attending she calls "Quilter's Choice" and the participants bring whatever they are working on. In the other, "Traditional Block," she instructs the participants in a particular pattern and over the course of the weekend everyone makes a small wall hanging–size quilt.

Sister Betty had invited us all to bring our sewing machines, but I had brought only the handwork with me that evening. I expected a retreat run by a Catholic nun to be sprinkled with lots of devotions and lectures drawing parallels between quilt making and our spiritual lives. This was part of the reason I had brought my handwork, thinking it lent itself more to listening and meditating. Also, the next project for my sewing machine was the binding on an otherwise finished quilt, not one of my favorite parts of quilt making.

For a small additional charge, participants can spend the night at Manna House. Since I live only a few miles away, I opted to return home in the evenings. I hadn't made the decision based on money. I was feeling guilty about signing up for the retreat in the first place. My younger son, Paul, was going to be home that weekend. He was about three weeks away from leaving the country with his National Guard unit. I knew even if

I stayed home he wouldn't be spending a lot of time with me, but I still felt I should be there to feed him if nothing else. I had, however, been wanting to attend one of Sister Betty's retreats for quite a while and had only learned of its schedule at the last minute. Even as I left the office, I was uncertain if I was doing the right thing.

I arrived to find the other three participants and Sister Betty already at their machines. Since I was the last quilter they were expecting, once I removed my coat and caught my breath, we all moved from the tables to a cozy lounge area where Sister Betty lead a brief prayer and devotion. We each introduced ourselves, and Sister Betty explained how the retreat worked. There were specific times for meals and we were all invited to Mass on Saturday evening or Sunday morning. Otherwise, we would quilt until we were tired, sleep, and then quilt again. Sister Betty explained that sometimes we would all be chattering away and other times we would be very quiet. This was normal as we each became absorbed in our tasks.

Betty's niece, who had attended the retreat several times, had very specific goals for the weekend. She was working on a Log Cabin quilt. She had the strips cut and was ready to begin piecing the blocks from the center outward. Her energy and enthusiasm were contagious. Since I was going home anyway, I decided I'd bring my machine back in the morning and tackle that binding project after all.

I was the first one to quit that evening. I had put in a long day at the office and knew I had a fifteen-minute drive and probably dirty dishes still ahead of me. I went home a little disappointed. I was feeling a need for some spiritual renewal and wondered if I was going to get it simply by sewing. I could sew at home.

When I arrived Saturday morning with my machine, queen-size quilt, and another basket of supplies, everyone was already sewing. They must have all gotten up early and eaten fast, I thought.

The other quilters offered some ideas on different methods of binding, and I went to work. I had some trouble because the backing and cover didn't fit exactly. Somewhere or other they hadn't been perfectly smooth when I'd pinned the layers together. Since I had tied the quilt instead of quilting it, this problem hadn't shown up until now. I had to rip my stitches out several times, at first using a pin because I had forgotten my seam ripper. Then Catherine Silhan, another repeat retreater, loaned me hers. I told her to let me know when she needed it back. I teased her later that it was disgusting how she stitched away the rest of the day without needing to redo anything. I used her seam ripper many times as I tried to ease the layers together with a minimum of puckers.

The frustration of the task, however, was eased by the good-natured sympathy of the other quilters and by the quilt talk going on around me. Everyone talked about quilts: what they were making, what they had finished, what they hoped to make in the future.

Some even talked about other gatherings of quilters. Sister Betty and her niece have other relatives who quilt. A small group of them get together for a weekend once a year. They make a quilt that they raffle off at the family reunion. It's easy to imagine the fun and difficulties of getting together with a group of sisters and cousins with the expressed purpose of making an entire quilt, first cut to last stitch, in just a couple of days. Not every family could do it. In my own family, it would become a test to see who really is the bossiest.

In Betty's family, someone's motto had been "shoot for good enough." Perhaps that kept the perfectionists from getting too critical of the rest. I decided the motto described my best chances with the binding. It was way too late for anything better, though it would, of course, still serve its purpose.

Our tables were in a semicircle near the walls to give us access to electrical outlets. The arrangement left a large open area in the center of the room to spread and arrange blocks. It also provided a place to spread out finished quilts for viewing. I finished my quilt and spread it out sometime in the early afternoon. In spite of the trouble with the binding, I was, and am, very pleased with the quilt. It's a variation on the Roman Square done in reds, rusts, and browns with a little bit of blue, all in leafy prints. And it's huge. I made it for a queen-size bed, and I like my quilts to have several inches of overhang. I decided that I would blame my difficulties with it on the fact that it is so large.

I returned to hand quilting for the rest of the afternoon, but it didn't fit the "sew as much as you can while you have the chance" attitude of my fellow quilters, which was contagious. I couldn't imagine spending all Sunday morning hand quilting. I kept thinking of all the other opportunities I would have to work on the Take Along quilt, since it travels so well. This retreat was my chance to do something I'd been putting off.

When I went home Saturday evening, I packed a new set of fabric I had been collecting. I wanted to make a quilt almost entirely of fat quarters. I knew I'd need to buy a few more fabrics to have enough, but I couldn't know how many until I had cut out a few blocks. I gathered all the supplies I'd need to start cutting out the pieces. I remembered to include a seam ripper this time, although I didn't expect to get far enough to do any actual sewing.

I tossed in a spool of white thread for one of the other quilters. She had worried that she was going to run out but hated to leave her sewing for a trip to the store. I had promised to bring her one from home since I was leaving anyway. It seemed an appropriate way to pay forward the favor of the loaned seam ripper.

Sunday morning I couldn't wait to get back to town and start on my quilt. We were all aware that we were down to our last few hours. Catherine was sorry she hadn't brought more to work on while Sister Betty and her niece were both pushing themselves to finish what they had planned to do over the weekend. Sister Betty joked that she would have to stay after class if she didn't get done. I felt a twinge of envy. I wanted to stay after class, too.

I cut 4-inch × 4-inch squares and large triangles, while I both fed from and added to the energy of the quilters around me. Being surrounded by people who share your interests affirms your own. Instead of feeling as though there was something else I should have been doing or feeling selfish for spending so much time on my hobby, I could accept that this quilting was what I was supposed to be doing at the moment. And with all these other joyful quilters around me, it seemed like the most wonderful and reasonable hobby there could be.

As I worked, I began planning for next year. I would see if Eden could join me. We might have to share my machine since hers is a cabinet model, and we would spend the night. That way, we could get in at least another hour of sewing each evening. Plus there was the fellowship at breakfast I had missed. We would definitely plan to spend the night.

Just before noon another sister came in and took group photos with the quilters' camera. I hadn't thought to bring one and made another mental note for next year. We shared one last meal, packed up our quilts, wished each other well, and headed home. On the way I realized that it truly had been a spiritually uplifting experience, more than any number of lectures would have been.

If I had spent the weekend in my own sewing room, I might have gotten some of the same stress-relief benefits, but the fellowship of other quilters was even more important. Without their affirmation of quilting, and by extension me as a quilter, I wouldn't have let everything else go and given myself over to a weekend of quilting. I actually noticed a decrease in the amount of stress I was feeling for several days after I returned to my demanding office work–housework–writing schedule. The retreat had definitely been the right thing for me to do.

Stitching Together

Quilters have known for a long time how important it is to have the backing of other quilters. Quilting bees in the late eighteenth and nineteenth centuries provided an isolated homemaker with an excuse to socialize. Fabric scraps and patterns were swapped along with the neighborhood gossip. The gatherings also served as support groups since the women were so often facing the same hardships.

The term *bee* was not intended to illustrate how busy the women were. Bee comes from *ben*, an Old English word meaning "help given by neighbors." Interestingly, *ben* can also mean "prayer," indicating the connection between spiritual thought and neighborly deeds, the spirituality of right conduct.

A true quilting bee worked a little like the threshing bees and husking bees in which everyone came together to get the harvesting done. It might have been an all-day affair. The hostess's quilt, waiting in the frame when the women arrived, would most likely have been finished when they left in the evening.

Out on the prairie, where neighbors were separated by many miles, men dropped the women off in the morning and came back to collect them in the evening. This made a fine excuse for the men to do a little socializing, as well. The hostess and another woman or two might leave the quilt frame a little early and prepare the food that each of the women had brought for the occasion.

A couple of superstitions that relate to social quilting during the nineteenth century involve problems that can still arise when you're quilting. If your thread broke, one superstition goes, you would have bad luck. Well, having the thread break is already bad luck. You have to pull out enough stitches to give yourself some thread to tie a knot, thread the tail back onto the needle, and bury it in the batting. Not fun.

The other superstition said that if your needle broke, you would be the next to have a baby. This seems particularly funny to us today because we picture quilting bees consisting primarily of older ladies. Remember, these were women of all ages, including young mothers and adolescent daughters. By the way, I broke two needles quilting my last hand-quilted project and it didn't get me any grandchildren, so it must not work if you skip a generation. Or maybe it didn't work because I was quilting alone.

During the Great Depression, quilting clubs were popular. These groups met for a few hours on a regular, sometimes weekly, basis. The location of the gathering rotated among the members' homes. If the hostess didn't have a quilt in her frame for everyone to work on, the women would bring their piecing to do as they visited.

The Persian Pickle Club (New York: St. Martin's Press, 1995), a novel by Sandra Dallas, uses one such club as the backdrop for a story about sisterhood. The husband of one of the members had bought a bolt instead of a yard of paisley fabric, which was also known as Persian pickle. Every quilt that any of the members make has some of that cloth in it. That shared fabric illustrates their shared joys and sorrows. With it and the other fabric they trade back and forth, they can see their friends in all the quilts. An unusual situation forces the members of the Persian Pickle Club to consider their conduct toward an outsider and one of their own and tests the sisterhood.

There were a few rules, which were somewhat common to most Depression-era quilting clubs. Confidences shared around the quilt frame weren't to be repeated outside the group. Possible new members were discussed within the group before they were invited, with the exception of the daughters of members, who were automatically members. The hostess, whose quilt was being stitched, would assign the women their places around the frame. The best quilters sat in the middle so their neat, tiny stitches would cover the areas that were most visible. Sitting at the frame at all was, in some clubs, an honor that had to be earned. A member might sit within the group, working on her own piecing until her skills became acceptable for the quilt in the frame.

After the Depression came World War II. Many more women began working outside the home, and fabric was less plentiful as more of the fabric manufacturers turned to making cloth for uniforms, parachutes, and other war-related textiles. Quilt making and quilting clubs became less popular. They didn't disappear entirely, however. Church groups have been primarily responsible for keeping both alive. The Amish in particular continued the old traditions and their quilt auctions still attract a great deal of attention.

In recent decades, new quilt groups have formed. They often call themselves guilds—the ancient term for an association of craftspeople. Generally a guild exists within a particular geographic area. The guild may be divided into smaller clubs or chapters, which may divide into still smaller groups that meet to sew. At least a few of these smallest groups call themselves bees after the old tradition.

The guilds host events such as seminars, workshops, and quilt shows. The chapters carry out their own activities, which often include some public service such as donating quilts to hospitals or raffling quilts as fundraisers for charity.

At the same time, more informal little groups have sprung up. These are simply friends who get together to enjoy fellowship with others that share a common interest in quilt making. The conduct of the members will determine whether the group is successful. A more experienced quilter who is convinced that her way is the only way can discourage beginners and spoil the fellowship. If the group works, it can provide an opportunity for all the quilters to learn from each other and a chance to share patterns, fabric scraps, and encouragement.

Several quilters I talked to cited socializing as their favorite part of quilt making. Many signed up for a class or quilted with a church group before quilting on their own, and mentioned meeting many nice people. When Mary Ellen Giglio wanted to learn to quilt, she decided it ought to be a family affair. She talked four of her six sisters and a couple of cousins into signing up for a class with her. She told them it would be a chance for them to spend time together. She in turn had been asked to the class by a coworker. Now Mary Ellen has dropped out along with one sister, too busy with small children to attend the class. But her sisters Teresa, Margaret, and Clara remain faithful.

Their mother had given all seven daughters sewing machines when they got married. None of the machines had gotten much use until the quilting class got them started. Now Mom is happy to see at least some of her girls using the machines.

A major benefit of a class seems to be the socializing, while a major benefit of the clubs is education. Most guilds have educational programs during part of their programs or offer workshops for beginners.

Marge Eaton belongs to the Capitol Quilters. Last year they put on a quilting demonstration at the Kansas State Historical Museum for National Quilt Day, the second Saturday in March, educating the public as well as each other. Marge also belongs to a less formal group that calls itself the TNT Quilters. TNT stands for Thursday Night Therapy, but they like to say that TNT Quilters are dynamite.

And, if two quilting organizations aren't enough, Marge tries to get to a quilt festival in California every year. There are classes, vendors, and exhibits all in some grand hotel. She visits a sister while she's there, but I don't think there's much question about why she's in California.

I don't belong to any of these clubs myself. I haven't been able to work them into my schedule. Perhaps that's why I enjoyed the retreat so much. It brought me together with other quilters for a time. Their love of the craft reinforced my own.

Stitched Together

Most everyone has heard of Amish quilts. In fact, quilting and the Amish are so closely associated in some peoples' minds that they believe the Amish are the only ones who still make quilts. Though that isn't quite true, their quilts did play a key role in reviving the current interest in quilts. Quilting continued in Amish society when it faded in the rest of the population in part due to their isolation. Avoiding modern conveniences kept them from turning to manufactured bedding. Another, probably more important factor, however, is their strong sense of community. The social aspects of quilting fit in well with their priorities.

At about the time of the U.S. bicentennial, there was a renewed interest in our country's past among the general population. Quilts are considered such a part of Americana that it isn't surprising there was a renewed interest in them as well. That is when the "outside world" discovered Amish quilts.

While Amish quilters produce quilts to sell, they also make them for their own use. Quilting has continued to be a community activity.

Intentional social isolation kept the old traditions alive for the Amish, while geographic isolation did the same for quilting in the Allegheny Mountain region of Appalachia. Poverty had a role as well, not so much in keeping women quilting, but in making them look for a way to sell their quilts and other handicrafts. In the 1960s, with their landscape destroyed by strip mining and suffering from unemployment rates three times the national average, a group of craftspeople in West Virginia formed The Mountain Artisans. The cooperative has been successful, expanding from quilted bedspreads to pieced garments and many other products.

The tricky part has been establishing a steady market for the products. Preserving the craft might have been a fundamental concern of some of the backers, but sales are what would ultimately preserve the cooperative. That's where the skirts and other products came in. But it all started with the quilting skills handed down through generations.

A cooperative called the Freedom Quilting Bee was started at about the same time in Gee's Bend, Alabama. In the 1840s, Mark Pettway, a plantation owner, moved his family and more than one hundred slaves from North Carolina to Gee's Bend. Many of the inhabitants of the community today are the descendants of those slaves.

Isolation and poverty are part of their lives, too, and their cooperative has suffered many of the same difficulties and setbacks as The Mountain Artisans. Their first set of quilts auctioned off in New York brought in less than $30 per quilt, a low return even in the 1960s. More recently, seventy of the community's quilts have formed a touring museum exhibit. The bold freedom of the quilt designs has been compared to improvisational jazz.

Quilting has always been a part of their lives, but it may not rescue them from poverty. Though the museum exhibit has revived several quilters' enthusiasm, whether this will revive the Quilting Bee cooperative remains to be seen. One of the Gee's Bend quilters compared the quilting gatherings to prayer meetings. It would be a shame if *that* should fade away.

Friendship Quilts

Back in the days when quilt making was a necessary household skill, *all* of your friends would have quilted. The activity would have meant more to some than to others, of course, but the fact that they all knew how to quilt made Friendship quilts possible.

If a woman were moving away, her friends would make a block of an agreed-on pattern. Each friend would stitch or write her name on the block. Some quilters used beautiful cross-stitched lettering while others followed the lines of their own handwriting with a narrow stem stitch. Or the quilters might have used indelible ink to write their names and other messages to the friend who was leaving.

The recipient of all these blocks would have put them together herself, perhaps forming friendships in her new community when she sought out women to help her with the actual quilting. Even though each block was made from the same pattern, the individuality of the quilters would still be apparent in the fabric choices, sewing skill, and especially in the autograph. Because of improvements in transportation, we don't have quite the sense of never seeing someone again if they move away. Still it was a beautiful tradition, and it's sad that it's been all but lost.

The Dresden Plate, pictured at the beginning of this chapter, was often the chosen pattern for Friendship quilts and is sometimes called a Friendship Ring because the center lends itself to the inclusion of a name. I autographed the center of one block in the Dresden Pate quilt I'm making as a nod to the old tradition.

groups, even though it's at a church other than her own. She wants to get some tips on hand quilting. An expert quilter uses a rocking motion to quilt, taking as many as ten stitches to the inch. This method, which is relatively fast once you get the hang of it, requires a frame. For a right-handed person, it's most natural to quilt from right to left. However, seated at a full-size frame, you need to be able to quilt in all directions in order to complete the quilt design in front of you. It is said that you don't really know how to quilt until you can quilt a complete circle without moving the quilt or yourself.

My freestanding hoop swivels. I don't even try to quilt backward. Nancy quilts without a frame, with the quilt on her lap, using running stitches. She doesn't know how to "rock."

When a section is quilted on a full-size frame, the quilters stop and roll the quilt to expose another section of the quilt. My hoop holds a section the right size for one quilter to reach. When it's done, I loosen the tension on the outside hoop, pop it off, and adjust the quilt (which is dragging on the floor) to a new section just for one. I don't get to "roll."

We're mostly solo quilters now. Even if we get together, we each work on our own projects. Our friends' stitches aren't part of our quilts, nor are we any tangible part of theirs. Perhaps it is part of our current culture that makes me want to be able to say of my quilts, "I did it all myself." I am also so short on free time I am reluctant to work on someone else's quilt, even if it means that I will eventually get help with my own. What if the club falls apart and we never get to mine? I'd be better off staying home and quilting alone with the TV.

But even so, I long for the backing of other quilters. I'm thrilled when I learn that some longtime acquaintance quilts, or I meet someone new and discover she's a quilter. We may not ever get together to share our quilting stories, but there's some sort of comfort in knowing there are other quilters out there.

Nancy Collins is a member of my church. Sometimes we bring our latest projects to church to show to each other and talk over particular problems. We've both been known to do a little stitching during Sunday school since our instructor, my husband, is patient with that type of thing. That may be the closest I'll ever come to a quilting club. But then again, one day I may decide I am simply missing out on too much by doing all my quilting alone.

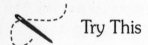 **Try This**

Make some quilting contacts if you don't already have some. Watch the newspaper for reports of programs at quilting guild meetings. Even if you don't feel you have the time to join a group, call and inquire about upcoming meetings and ask if they allow guests. Often retreats and classes are open to the public and represent less of a time commitment, if that's the issue. Just being around other quilters can be encouraging and inspiring.

chapter seven

All You Need
Is Love

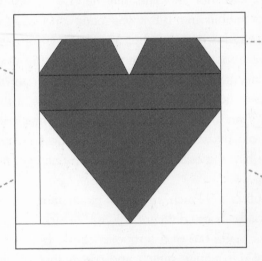

Assemble Your Quilt

Spread your backing on the floor, right-side down. Smooth your batting over it and your quilt cover over the batting. Begin at the center and pin the layers together with large safety pins no more than 8 inches apart. If you'll be quilting, baste the layers together once you're sure there are no wrinkles. Begin at the center and work outward until the quilt is covered with lines of basting stitches no more than 4 or 5 inches apart. Remove the pins, flip the whole thing over, and smooth it out to make sure there aren't any wrinkles or puckers on the backing side. Replace stitches if you need to. Doesn't it look and feel like a real quilt?

Love in Every Stitch

It was made sometime in the late 1950s, so it isn't really an antique, at least not yet. The only hand stitching on it is the backside of the binding. But it was made especially for my husband, Joe, by his grandmother Minnie Swenson Benson. He has recollections of seeing the fabric when the work was in progress. His grandmother's little green house near the library was always so tidy; it seemed strange to see piles of cloth on the bed in the spare bedroom and on her sewing machine. He isn't sure how old he was, but he makes a guess at twelve. She didn't give him the quilt, however, until he and I were married in 1973.

The quilt is a 9-Patch, mostly of gingham checks and coordinating solids. These different colored 9-Patch blocks alternate with blocks made out of a turquoise check. Blocks made with fabrics that don't quite match and pieces that are cut on the bias, throwing the lines of checks into odd angles, testify to the fact that her 9-Patch blocks were made from scraps, some of which were too small for her to cut her patch straight with the grain. There are a few plaids instead of checks and a couple of blocks with a black-checked piece in the center square because she ran out of pink or red, but she managed to match her scraps enough that the pattern is still recognizable as a 9-Patch.

The binding is a turquoise fabric with pink and yellow flowers. I suspect it was also made from what she had on hand. In fact, my guess is the only new components were the backing and the repeating turquoise-checked fabric. I would not be surprised to discover the batting is made from an old blanket, although I could be wrong. I don't plan to take it apart to see.

The quilt's value on the market would be sadly low. Its value to Joe is enormous. Grandma Benson thought of Joe and his future when she sewed those squares together and then followed the seams to quilt it with her sewing machine. Joe thinks of his grandmother and his past when he uses the quilt. It's kept on a quilt rack in our bedroom and is tossed onto the bed on especially cold nights or called into service for an afternoon nap.

At about the same time that Joe's grandmother was making his quilt, or possibly a few years earlier, Rick's grandmother was making the quilt he now owns and cherishes. Rick Cairns is a heating and air-conditioner service technician. I've gotten acquainted with him during the past couple of years because his boss is married to my boss and both businesses are run out of the same office. Rick is not the type of guy you would expect to be particularly sentimental. However, this middle-aged, divorced Vietnam veteran worries that he's not storing his grandmother's quilt properly. I get the impression it may be his most prized possession.

The quilt is a wonderful example of an Improved 9-Patch. This is a more complicated version of a 9-Patch in which the outside corners of the four corner squares of each block extend outward from the block. The spaces between the blocks are pointed ovals of the same white fabric as the four alternate squares in the 9-Patch.

Rick's grandmother's quilt is completely hand stitched, from piecing to quilting to binding. His grandmother didn't do all the quilting, however. She belonged to a quilting circle, and Rick remembers the women seated around the quilt frame at his grandmother's house. Though this particular quilt wasn't made especially for him, he remembers his grandmother getting her quilts out for him to look at and asking which one he liked best. "It was always this one," he says.

There's something about these grandmothers' quilts that can make these strong men misty. They were quilts made by women they loved and given to them as a visible sign of a love for them they never had reason to doubt. What better legacy is there than that?

Full-size quilts, like the ones Joe and Rick inherited, are seldom, if ever, used. Neither of these men would want to think of their quilts being worn-out. I don't believe this is uncommon. Quilts represent too much work, for one thing, and are treasured because of the woman who did all that work. But also, they aren't really needed. Blankets are cheap and accessible. It's hard to imagine falling on such hard times that we would need to use these treasured keepsakes.

But baby quilts are another matter. Babies can go through so many blankets between washdays that every blanket available is liable to get called into service. Besides, we want everything to be perfect for the little one and might switch to heavier or lighter blankets several times a day.

We also have a baby quilt that Joe's Grandma Benson made. I'm not as sure of its history, but I think it was made for Joe as well, about the time he was born. Joe's mother used it with both her boys and passed it on to us before our first child was born. It's a Split 9-Patch in the Double X arrangement. Each block is made from a different print and a coordinating solid. Again, one blue triangle that should have been red and a couple of triangles that were pieced together from two scraps illustrate Grandma Benson's frugality.

The backing is a cute pink and blue print with puppies playing among balloons and butterflies. The same fabric binds the edges. The poor thing has been washed enough that the edges are starting to fray. The next mother and father to get the quilt may face the decision to replace the binding or retire the quilt. I will respect either decision. Grandma Benson lived to be ninety-three so all three of our children had a chance to know and love her. They will see the quilt for more than just its actual appearance, though it may be relegated to protecting the carpet from Baby or protecting Baby from the lawn.

Like Joe's grandmother and Rick's, it is often out of a desire to give that inspires quilters to make a quilt. The announcement of a baby on the way is especially conducive to quilt making. Part of this is simply our natural love of babies. A baby's most basic needs are food, shelter, and love. A quilt can symbolically provide two of these needs. We also like to make baby quilts because of our confidence that our quilt's imperfections will be more readily overlooked in a baby quilt.

If you're a beginning quilter, a baby quilt is a great place to start because it will be small—with fewer pieces to cut and stitch together, progress will be fast. To me, the hardest part of quilt making is getting layers together smoothly, as my problems with the binding on the quilt I finished at the retreat illustrate. This is much easier to do with a smaller quilt.

In fact, the first nine quilts I made were crib- or lap-robe–size quilts, and they were each made with one particular person in mind. It took me awhile to get up the courage to tackle a full-size quilt. Besides, there are so many darling flannel and cotton children's prints available that mix and match and just beg to be quilted. But then, usually, the fabric inspires me.

When we are making a quilt for some special person, we aren't imagining it being wrapped in acid-free tissue paper and stored away in a cedar chest. We get a lot of pleasure out of thinking about the person who will receive the finished quilt and of imagining them using it.

My daughter says she is excited about the prospect of making quilts as gifts. She finds herself wishing that one friend would get married so she could make her something out of some colors she has seen and knows her friend would love. Or she thinks another friend has to have another baby so she can make her family something. Even though she has been sewing less than a year, Eden has already made an appliquéd pillow for a friend and tiny quilted tree ornaments as Christmas gifts.

Several quilters mentioned the quilts they had made for other people before the ones they made for themselves, finding a special pleasure in those quilts. Nearly all the Picture quilts and Memory quilts mentioned in earlier chapters were made as gifts.

Lillian Ruud has made quilts for all her grandchildren and is now making them for her great-grandchildren. She says she wouldn't mind getting a quilt or two ahead, perhaps thinking of a day when she can no longer quilt. Eunice Borman made full-size quilts for all her grandchildren and has moved on to baby quilts for her hoped-for great-grandchildren.

Lillian, Eunice, and I are happy to make quilts commemorating events that have yet to happen. We are confident that someone will use our creations. We use these hoped-for babies as an excuse to keep making quilts. Others, like Eden, want to tailor their quilts for someone special or don't have extra time to quilt any "maybe if" quilts.

Considering the amount of time it takes to make a quilt, especially if the piecing or quilting is done by hand, it might seem amazing how many quilters love to give them away. Catherine Silhan made a quilt for each of her nephews and one for a cousin. Kristy J. Kahrs writes that giving quilts away is one of her favorite parts of quilt making. "It's really great to give them as gifts and see people's reaction." Eden's friend Sarah Croco cites wanting to make gifts for people as her reason for wanting to learn to quilt.

Kathryne Perney got a clear picture of just how many quilts she has given away when she got out her quilt diaries to show someone else. She has four volumes now. "You don't have *this* many quilts" was the comment. "No, I've given most of them away," she said. Her four-volume quilt diary holds a clue to why prolific quilters love to give their quilts away. If they kept them all, they would eventually have all they needed and have to stop.

But some quilters make the gifts before they've made quilts for themselves. Vic Koch likes to quilt but hasn't had a lot of time. The only full-size quilt she's made was a graduation gift for a niece. She made it in Kansas State University's colors, purple and white, and the niece loved it. She was pleased to tell me it was being used. She knew her niece well enough to know what she would like and loved her enough to go to the work of making it. There are many things Vic might have chosen to make or buy for a young woman embarking on a new phase of her life. A quilt offered love and shelter, both needed as much at this time as they were when she was a baby.

Julie Koch says that whenever she got homesick or missed her family, she could cuddle up in the quilt and think about all the fun times she'd had with Vic and her family. She made her bed every day so people would be sure to see the quilt. After she graduated from college, she got a larger bed and the quilt became a throw for winter TV watching. She intends to keep the quilt as long as she can, cherishing it because it was made by someone special and, as she concludes, "came from the heart."

The choice of the school colors for the quilt may have had a subtle meaning. They are both aware of the quilt being from one K-State fan to another. Julie says purple is her favorite color *because* she's such a fan and Vic was also catering to her niece's preferences. But the school colors combined with the fact that the girl was going away to college showed the aunt's support of Julie's choices. Vic, an elementary school teacher, is proud to see her young relatives pursue higher education.

For many quilters, while there's joy in simply quilting, that alone isn't enough to provide the enthusiasm needed to complete the task. As Bonnie mentioned in reference to the Picture quilts she loves to make and give away, you need to have a connection with the person you're quilting for. Marge Eaton agreed to make a quilt for an acquaintance. Ten years later she turned the unfinished quilt over to her daughter to finish. She could never really get her heart into a quilt that wasn't special to her.

If you have a relationship with the recipient, it affects the quilt, in the colors and patterns you choose, because you want to please the recipient, but also in the care you take with the construction. The quilt may explicitly reflect the event you are celebrating, as is the case with so many Picture quilts, or the event may simply provide the stimulus to get you quilting. Although a quilt that commemorates a milestone will be remembered as part of the event, a quilt made without an event, simply out of love, is like an enormous thinking-of-you card.

While our relationships affect our quilts, quilts we give as gifts have an impact on the relationship. Few people can receive a gift that clearly took many hours and not be moved. We may not love someone more because they gave us a quilt, or anything else for that matter. Our affection isn't bought that easily. But if they *make* us a quilt, it's a little hard to ignore their affection for us.

I haven't made any full-size quilts as gifts yet. There are still a few beds in my house that don't have the full complement of quilts. By that I mean one lightweight quilt for summer and one made with the extra-thick batting for winter. A medium-weight quilt would be good, too, come to think of it. Meanwhile, most any quilt that my children take a liking to they're welcome to take home. Though none of my children are exactly "settled" yet, they don't live here, either. They can take a bit of this home with them, if they want. That just gives me an excuse to make more quilts.

A Touch of Home

Making quilts for new brides is an old tradition based on the same sort of offering of love and shelter as baby quilts. The quilt also offers implicitly a blessing on the most intimate part of a young couple's relationship and a wish that the couple be blessed with children. In pioneer days, a young woman was expected to learn to sew at an early age and have a baker's dozen, or thirteen, quilts completed before she was married.

One enthusiastic quilter I met is determined to make thirteen quilts for each of her two children before they get married. She's going to count baby quilts, she notes. Even so, that would set a young couple up with bedding for quite a while.

Thirteen quilts seem like a lot for today, but in an earlier era, houses weren't heated the way they are now and it would take more than one to keep the couple warm in the winter. Running a household, being responsible for all the baking and washing, as well as raising babies would cut into a young woman's quilting time for several years. Also, quilts were used as room dividers in the little log cabins some of these brides moved into. Quilts were hung on walls for the same reasons that tapestries were hung on the walls of medieval castles: to add beauty and to cut down on drafts. Thinking about it, thirteen would be barely enough, especially if she had several children before she found time to make some more.

The guidebooks for westward travelers in the nineteenth century recommended two or three blankets or comforters per person. Most of the coverings taken were probably quilts. The same guidebooks, however, mention the use of blankets for simple tents and for litters. I doubt if two or three would be enough. The best quilts were used to cushion breakable items such as china and glass during the journey. Everyday quilts were folded on wagon seats to take a little of the pain out of riding over the rough trails on the hard wooden benches. Quilts were hung for privacy and for windbreaks to keep the blowing dust out of the wagons. Quilts were slept on and under in the wagon box or on the bare ground. Some were worn-out before they reached their destination. The ones that survived gave their owners a much-needed sense of home.

Sadly, quilts were also used in place of coffins. On parts of the trail, wood was too scarce to find to build a coffin and time was limited, besides. Many a hapless victim of disease or accident was laid to rest wrapped in a quilt. It may have given the family members some comfort to know that though their loved one was left behind, he or she was encircled with something that clearly symbolized home and family.

Even in settled communities of the time, quilts offered comfort when a loved one died. Bodies were laid out for viewing on quilts. Occasionally coffins were draped with a quilt during a funeral service. Before commercial coffin liners, family members might make a quilt for that purpose. For a while when photography was relatively new, photographing a deceased infant was popular. The child was either laid in bed or in his mother's arms as if he were asleep. Often there was a quilt either under or over the child.

In times joyous or tragic, few things say love and family quite the way a quilt can.

Love Magic

The old superstitions involving quilts further illustrate their importance to the homemaker. Most of these superstitions were common during the Victorian era although their origin is probably much older. Some were still, if not entirely believed, at least repeated well into the twentieth century. For example, a person who was ill should sleep under a quilt because the love from that quilt would help him mend faster. The first person to sleep under a new quilt would have her dreams come true. Imagine a doctor or psychologist prescribing new quilts for physical or emotional well-being.

Another example was the notion that a husband or teenage son should never be allowed to sleep under a quilt called Wandering Foot for fear he would get the wanderlust and leave. Some thought the pattern became safe when it was renamed Turkey Tracks, but others still shunned it. But then again,

Wandering Foot is an appliqué pattern that looks sort of hard to make. The superstition might have offered an added excuse for not attempting it. It's enough for me, I'm afraid.

Most of the superstitions involved a young woman's chances of finding a mate. For instance, it was considered bad luck for a girl to put a heart shape on her quilt until she was actually engaged. It was bad luck to begin a quilting project and not complete it. That unfinished quilt was surely the reason a young woman wasn't being asked to marry. Good thing I was already married when I started the Cathedral Window quilt eighteen years ago. It still isn't completely finished.

If you wrapped an unmarried woman in a quilt when it was just off the frame, she would have good luck at finding a mate. If a young woman threw a quilt that was just off the frame around a single man, it would charm him into a relationship with her. I can see how that one might actually work. What's he doing hanging around during a quilting bee if he isn't interested in some young woman, anyway?

If an unmarried woman shook a quilt out the front door, the next unmarried man to cross the threshold would be the one she would marry. This last seems a little risky. I'd imagine the young woman would try to be sure she knew who was expected before she shook the quilt or she would have stepped out into the yard to do it, which may have been the point of the superstition. "Go on out in the yard," says Mom. "You're blowing the dust back into the house. Don't be so lazy or I'll marry you off to the next ne'er-do-well who walks through that door."

A game cat lovers will frown on was Shake the Cat. Four unmarried girls would put a cat on a quilt. They would lift the quilt, one girl at each corner, and shake it. Whichever girl was closest to the cat when it jumped off would be the next to be married. Imagine the poor cat as the girls rowdily tried to manipulate which way it would jump.

One superstition that had two opposite versions involved who took the last stitch on a quilt that was being stitched with other quilters. One version said she'd be the next to marry. The other said she would be an old maid. Whether this was regional or varied to suit the participants is unknown.

For a young woman to start her thirteenth quilt before she was actually engaged would have been bad luck. It was the Bride quilt and was made between the engagement and the wedding. She might choose to make a Wedding quilt, which would feature the names of the intended couple and the date of their wedding perhaps inside a heart of appliquéd flowers or some similar fancy work. Or it might have been one of the many pieced patterns that were popular Bride quilts like True Lover's Knot, a pieced work of interlocking squares, or Honeymoon Cottage, a pieced house that probably took on many different forms, or Bridal Stairway. This last is a series of rectangular steps, which surround a center on-point square. The effect is sort of steps zigzagging across the quilt.

What the prospective bride made would depend on her skill and the amount of time she had. This quilt would be her "best quilt" and would be brought out occasionally, perhaps to deco-rate the parlor during some special event but never used unless her family fell on hard times. To be reduced to using the good quilts for everyday, as Marguerite Martin used the Lone Star during the Depression, was sad, indeed. Having a good quilt or two put away symbolized prosperity.

Our old quilts—whether we've gotten them from a grandmother, aunt, or other loved one—mean more to us than simply cloth stitched together to make a blanket. They represent love. They represent the life of the one who made them. They are a legacy of love.

Stand By Your Quilter

The legacy continues, of course, with our own quilts, but the people who live with an avid quilter don't always see it in such romantic terms. More than one bewildered husband has called his wife a "crazy quilter," and he wasn't referring to the type of quilts the woman was making. It seems to be the little things that bother these guys the most. Little things like tiny threads all over the wife's clothes when they go out together because she ran to the sewing room to stitch together one more row of blocks before it was time to leave. Or worse yet, the tiny threads that are all over *his* clothes because he sat on the couch where she had been sewing the night before.

Or little things like needles and pins are even worse. Especially when family members find them with their bare feet. Socks aren't much better. And the quilter is more thrilled to find the missing needle than she is concerned about the bleeding.

Having piles of projects on the floor of the living room or on the kitchen table takes some getting used to, as does having to have enough light to sew by whenever they are watching TV together or sewing machine noise in a small apartment, sometimes lasting into the night.

Every quilter is confident that she can train her cohabitants not to eat or drink on the bed without removing the quilt first. Some have been more successful than others.

Bonnie says her family should appreciate the fact that she quilts because it keeps her at home and out of the malls. Sometimes they may feel as if she is no more accessible when she's shut away in her sewing room than if she weren't home. But they do know where she is.

And she didn't mention fabric stores. When I called to interview one of the quilters for this book, I got her husband. "The fabric store called so she's gone for the morning," he said. I don't believe she got an actual phone call from the fabric store. I think the call was on a more spiritual level than that.

The hardest thing for husbands of quilters, though, is probably the questioning. "Should this be turned this way or that?" "Which fabric goes the best?" and worst of all, "Do you think this works?"

Wives of male quilters probably don't have quite the same problem. Men are less likely to ask these questions unless they really want their wife's opinion. Women, on the other hand, are more likely to be thinking out loud and asking for reassurance. No answer is really going to help, least of all, honesty. If she does what he suggests and doesn't like the quilt when it's done, guess whose fault that was. Evasive answers might work, if he's good at that type of thing. Saying, "I'm sure whatever you decide will be fine" may seem like a safe answer, but to her he's saying he doesn't care about this quilt, her favorite hobby, or by extension, her.

My recommendation to husbands is to ask her what she thinks is wrong or what isn't working. Keep asking questions until she's talked herself through her problem and arrived at a solution; then immediately agree. If she says, "I couldn't have done it without you," he's welcome to take all the credit he wants.

But that, of course, is also his cue to leave her to her quilting. Quilts may be made with love in every stitch, but a thread's going to break and pop a seam every now and then. It's best to mend them as quickly as possible.

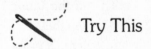 Try This

Make the reverse of a Friendship quilt. Instead of collecting blocks from your friends, make a single block that represents one of your friends. Choose the fabric carefully with that person in mind. Think about what this person's friendship means to you, and choose or design a pattern that makes you think of the person. Incorporate something that symbolizes your friend's talents and interests. Send loving thoughts his or her way as you stitch the block. Quilt it and bind it and make it into a hanging. Present it to your friend without waiting for a particular occasion.

chapter eight

Let Not Your Heart Be Troubled

The Quilting Stitch

Quilting stitches hold the layers together. With the quilt in a hoop or frame, use short needles called "betweens" and quilting thread to take tiny stitches along your marked lines. With practice, you can "rock" the needle in and out, controlling it with pressure from your thimble-covered third finger against the eye end of the needle. The middle finger of your off hand under the quilt stops the needle's downward motion, and the thumb of your upper hand presses the quilt down ahead of the needle. Remind yourself that it doesn't have to be perfect. A few little errors aren't going to be noticeable, and even accomplished quilters take out a few stitches from time to time.

A Stitch in Time

Whatever your quilting method might be—by hand, sewing machine, or quilting machine—you have to choose a design or pattern for those stitches. There are three basic types of quilting designs, and, I have decided, there are three basic types of quilt makers.

This is not to say that one type of quilter is more likely to choose the quilting design that corresponds to their approach to quilt making over the other designs. Most of the time, we all try to choose the design that fits our quilt. This is just a funny little correlation I came upon while quilting one day. If part of the aim of Zen is to know yourself, it might be instructive to consider which type of quilter you are.

The first type of quilt design (and quilter) is the patch-by-patch approach. With this design, the quilting stitches follow the pieces of the quilt, generally ¼ inch inside the seam line of every piece. This is a clear and methodical way to quilt and is ideal for complicated pieced quilts. It shows off the design of the quilt pattern to good effect. One way to keep it from becoming boring is to quilt a second outline inside the first on the larger pieces or quilt an X through some of them.

A patch-by-patch quilter is going to make her quilts one at a time. She will nearly always have one quilt under way but won't start a new one until she has finished the last. This, also, is a methodical approach and is ideal for some quilters, especially if they make the more complicated quilts. One way to keep it from getting boring is to try new patterns and look forward to the next adventure.

A second quilting design alternates simple background stitch patterns, such as crosshatches on the busier areas of the quilt, with fancier stitch patterns such as a feathered wreath on the more open areas. This is ideal for quilts in which pieced or appliquéd blocks alternate with plain, solid color blocks or on appliquéd quilts that have one design that spreads across the quilt, leaving some blank spaces.

A background-stitches quilter quilts in the background of her life. Quilt making is one of several hobbies, and once in a while, she decides to make a quilt. In between she does other things. This is ideal for the creative person who alternates creative outlets.

The third basic quilting style is the all-over motif. This is a quilting design that repeats over the entire quilt, disregarding seam lines. This adds continuity to sampler designs and draws attention away from the blocks themselves by emphasizing the effect of the blocks as they blend together. This can be something regulated like clamshells or random like meandering.

The all-over quilter has several projects going at once, sometimes all over the house. Whatever suits today's mood is the quilt that gets attention today, regardless of which quilt was started first. This draws attention away from the individual quilts (product) by emphasizing the art of quilt making itself (process). There can be artificial restrictions (I set my limit at five) or the sky's the limit.

A Time to Stitch

The quilting stitch is the one thing that scares away the most
would-be quilters. When she was first getting started, Joyce
Swenson became frustrated at the difficulty of finding anyone to
teach her the quilting stitch. Nancy Collins and Barbara Booth
both developed their own version by quilting without a hoop or
a frame. Some quilters will put their quilt in a hoop but use a
stab-and-pull kind of stitch. These all get the job done, but
hoopless quilting is a little more puckered than traditional
quilting. Stab-and-pull stitches are larger and more crooked.
Danny McReynolds ties his quilts or turns them over to his
mother-in-law to quilt for him.

A good teacher or instruction book and the willingness to
practice might make it easier for any of these folks. I think it's
worth a try. The quilting stitch is part of the beauty of traditional
quilts—and of not-so-traditional quilts. Kathryne Perney does
all her quilting on a long-arm machine. It's her favorite part of
quilt making. "Quilting is like the frosting on the cake," she said.
"It brings the quilt to life."

The stitch was originally developed to keep the batting from
shifting. Before there was commercial batting, quilts were
stuffed with squares of combed cotton, wool, flax, or linen that
were laid side-by-side on top of the backing. As you can
imagine, the rows of stitching had to be within an inch or so of
each other to keep these squares in place.

Nowadays, unless a quilt gets some very hard use, the batting isn't going to shift much as long as the spaces between the

rows of stitching aren't more than 4 or 5 inches. In fact, some batting packages will tell you how close your stitching should be for that particular batting.

Plain quilts, sometimes called Whole Cloth quilts, like the block illustrated at the beginning of this chapter, are quilts made of one solid color. The only decoration on the quilt is the elaborate quilting stitches. They were popular for a while in the post–Victorian era, causing women to flip their patchwork quilts over so they would look as if they were Plain.

The Amish, who are given much credit for saving quilt making from obscurity when it fell out of favor with much of the rest of the population, perfected the Plain quilt. They came to quilt making relatively late, choosing instead to make German-style coverlets until around 1870. The conservative colors— browns, blues, and black—that they used reflected their affinity for simplicity. However, the stitching they did on these Plain quilts was incredibly detailed.

Imagine trying to quilt on a dark fabric. The white thread would really show up, which is good news and bad news. You'd be able to see what you were doing, but so would everyone else. Every oversize or crooked stitch would stand out in stark relief.

I have too much fun with color combinations and lively prints to be interested in making a Plain quilt. But any quilt is going to benefit from careful quilting. There are alternatives to hand quilting, such as machine quilting or tying, but don't be too quick to eliminate hand quilting as a possibility.

Even if you don't have a group of quilters to help, you can still hand quilt a full-size quilt. Several quilters I interviewed said they get their quilting done a little at a time. They take a few minutes while something's in the oven or while waiting for their husband to be ready to go out. It takes awhile, but it does get done. Joyce Swenson says she gets the tops done in pretty good time; then they have to wait until she has time to quilt them.

And don't let the lack of a frame slow you up either. There are freestanding hoops that are relatively inexpensive on up to amazing contraptions that do just about everything but quilt for you. There are also hoops no bigger than standard embroidery hoops that are designed to hold the layers of a quilt. With some practice, you can learn to rock the needle while you balance the hoop against your body. This is what I'm using for my Take Along quilt.

The quilting stitch is the most repetitive phase of quilt making. With the exception of some hand-pieced or appliquéd patterns, it is also the most time-consuming. This is why our foremothers called in their friends to help. Of course in those days, they were probably putting two or three times as many quilting stitches into a quilt as we would now. Most of us like the lighter, fluffier look of a quilt whose stitches aren't quite so dense.

Quilting alone with the TV off, perhaps some soft music playing to block out the more distracting sounds of the world, is ideal for meditation. The quilting stitch is a slow, smooth motion. It requires concentration to keep the stitches straight and even.

This concentration prevents you from dwelling on your immediate worries, so it calms your nerves and becomes, even if you aren't consciously trying, a form of meditation. This is the phase of quilt making most conducive to "flow" or being "in the zone," that wonderful place where all that exists is what you are doing right at that moment. Rock to the right, press down with the thumb, and rock the needle upright again. All that exists is the line of stitching. Even burying knots and cutting new lengths of thread are done with that same slow, smooth motion. It's almost dreamlike.

It's somewhat mysterious how this extreme concentration on the task of the moment somehow takes us out of ourselves at the same time. Of course, this can be true of any phase of quilt making once you become confident enough in the process that you're no longer worried about doing it wrong but still need to remain aware on a certain level of what you are doing. Using the sewing machine to piece or quilt can do this for a lot of people. Quilt making works better than garment construction for meditation, I believe, because of the repetition that is necessary. With any other sewing, you move on to a new type of task too quickly.

The quilting stitch itself seems somehow to lend itself naturally to this flow that comes with the right concentration. I don't know whether it's difficult for me to bring my worries with me to the quilt frame or whether I simply can't stay at the quilt frame for more than a few minutes if I don't leave my worries behind. It may be that I become too restless to sit still if I have too many other things on my mind. I have heard quilters talk of times when they simply couldn't quilt. Their stitches were too uneven. I suspect they were having trouble getting out of themselves and into the quilting.

Perhaps I have conditioned myself to drop my worries very quickly when I start to stitch. I may intentionally head for my quilting when I need to escape. I have noticed myself relaxing almost immediately.

Other quilters' stories support this theory. Teresa LaFlair says that she finds peace while quilting. In fact, with her hectic family life and job at a jail, the quilting class she attends some-times seems like the only peace she has. Kathryne Perney agrees. "It's just you, the quilting machine, and the quilt," she says. She deals with issues that are bothering her and has made decisions or solved problems while quilting. Even after her quilting moved from a hobby to a business, in which she quilts for others on her long-arm machine, she still recognizes quilting as a stress reliever.

Prescription to Quilt

Several quilters referred to their quilt making as therapy and their quilting club or class as their support group. Marge Eaton's group is even called Thursday Night Therapy. For some quil-ters, this goes beyond the benefits of social interaction and a little R and R. Sharon Fields calls her classes a "healing time" for members. Bonnie described an all-day headache that faded a few minutes into class.

In fact, when I've taken blocks of my Take Along quilt with me to the doctor's office and quilted even for just a few minutes before going back to the examining room, my blood pressure has been lower than is normal for me. Reading, or even knitting or crocheting, doesn't seem to work quite the same for me. I suspect it has something to do with that smooth motion. Maybe I knit and crochet too fast. Maybe my body reacts to what I am reading, and I leave my problems behind only to take on new ones vicariously. Whatever the reason, quilting lowers my blood pressure when these other activities do not.

But how can this really work? Studies have shown that meditation slows the production of cortisol, the body's stress hormone. It also slows metabolism in the red blood cells and alters activity in the sympathetic nervous system, which controls the body's involuntary functions, such as heart rate. Because of these physiological benefits, meditation was endorsed by the National Institutes of Health as far back as 1984 in a report on hypertension.

And these studies continue. Heart surgery patients at Columbia Presbyterian Medical Center in New York City are offered a program that includes meditation. Those who accept generally benefit from the reduced anxiety. But it has also been noted that these patients manage pain better and even have less operative bleeding.

I think these studies and their results are significant, but I also think it'll be a long time before Western culture embraces meditation as medical treatment. We want quickly seen, easily measured results. I suspect it is something we each have to experience for ourselves to believe.

I haven't actually tried formal sitting meditation in the waiting room at my doctor's office. I suspect that it wouldn't be

considered acceptable behavior in small-town Kansas, unless I
could make it look as if I were taking a nap. Quilting, though
not exactly common in that setting, is at least understood.

Sharon Fields believes quilt making helped her when she
was recovering from surgery. While she was recuperating, she
made each of her children a bright colored quilt. Until then, she
had generally chosen darker colors for her quilts. She had a
feeling while she was finishing the bright quilts that her dark
period was behind her. I think this may have been a way of
expressing through her quilting what many people feel after a
serious illness: a new appreciation of life.

Not everyone is going to have a meditative, relaxing experience the minute they begin to quilt. You have to learn the
quilt-making skills enough to do them automatically first. And
even after that, there has to be some intentional meditation
involved, at least at first. You can't just sit down at the quilt
frame and expect all your troubles to disappear. You need to
deliberately focus your attention on your stitches. Nancy
Collins doesn't consider quilting relaxing, but she admits she
puts pressure on herself to finish. My friend Linda who chose
a difficult pattern to begin with didn't find anything relaxing
about it, either.

Of course, even if you learn to escape into your quilting, all
your troubles are still there when you quit stitching. They should
be back in their proper perspective, though, and you should be
refreshed and more ready to cope with them. Admittedly, sometimes it doesn't work, but anyone who practices sitting meditation will tell you there are times when thoughts intrude. It takes

practice. It takes one more of the Zen keys to happiness; it takes right concentration.

Wrong concentration occurs when we dwell on things we can't do anything about or obsess over past failures or slights. Right concentration is more in the moment in touch with our creative selves.

Nearly every quilter I talked to spoke of needing a creative or artistic outlet. Clara MacDougall said that about four years ago, she was told she needed to get in touch with her creative side. She actually was given a prescription to quilt by a clergyman/councilor, who also told her she needed more social involvement. A quilting class filled both needs.

Several quilters are extremely creative, counting quilt making among many other creative hobbies. At least one paints; several sew and knit. Some have particular fun combining quilt making with another hobby. Cat lovers put cats on their quilts. Gardeners are drawn to flower or even vegetable prints. Danny McReynolds, an active 4-H supporter and leader, made a quilt with fabric with 4-H and clover prints.

Barbara Booth also draws. Recently she has transferred her drawings onto quilts. Instead of embroidering the picture as several of us have done with other people's drawings, she used it for her quilting lines. Using quilting thread, she worked a stem stitch through all the layers, putting the picture on both sides of her quilt.

Eunice Borman's husband recently retired from the Kansas Highway Patrol. They had collected Highway Patrol uniform shoulder patches from all fifty states. She put them all onto a

quilt, backed by two shades of blue. I wonder if she feels particularly safe sleeping under all those Highway Patrol patches.

Combining other hobbies with quilting is nothing new.
During more affluent times at the end of the nineteenth century
and the beginning of the twentieth, quilters put their collections
into what we now call Novelty quilts. One of the strangest to us
today was made with cigar ribbons. Cigars were often sold in
bundles tied with a silk ribbon. Because there were so many
cigar makers, there was keen competition. They stamped or
wove their company's name into the ribbons. Women began
collecting ribbons and stitching them onto a muslin backing to
make tablecloths and other home decorations.

Cigarette companies included sports trading cards in their
products to attract more customers. Around 1920 they decided
a small silk or cotton flannel picture in their packs might
increase their appeal to women. They used flags, butterflies,
college pennants, and Native American motifs among others.
These promotions were traded among the collectors and many
found their way into Novelty quilts.

When my family and I were going through some of my
dad's things after he died, we found a box of his fair ribbons.
Most of them are dated between 1929 and 1932. One of his
great-granddaughters, Kaylan Jones, now a college student, sug-
gested making the ribbons into a wall-hanging quilt. She and
I divided the ribbons. Kaylan could make a good-size quilt with
her own fair ribbons, and I've got quite a few as well. But Dad's
ribbons, going back to his high school and 4-H days, are special.

My half are still in a box, though I've set aside a couple of remnants of old flour sacks that I think will complement the old ribbons. I haven't decided how I want to turn his collection into a quilt. When I talked to Kaylan about the ribbons at a recent family reunion, she had gotten no farther than I. A reverence toward the ribbons has slowed us both down. We worry about ruining the fragile ribbons in our effort to display them. But also, these ribbons look old. It's going to take just the right arrangement and complementary fabrics to make it look charming rather than dowdy.

Permission to Quilt

We are all creative people, whether we are aware of it or not. It is part of human nature. It is a gift from the Creator, the part of ourselves that is in the image of God. We are giving thanks when we use our creativity. We are not being selfish. Society has conditioned us to think our hobbies should wait until all the work is done. Unless our creativity benefits someone else or earns us money, it is self-indulgent. This may account for some of the gift giving that quilters enjoy so much. It makes it all right for them to be creative.

Anyone who believes he is not creative or lacks imagination was taught to believe that. Someone, a teacher or a parent perhaps, criticized some tender effort, leaving him overly critical of himself. This is tragic. Without creativity, we feel powerless. Our imagination is what makes us dream, and dreams are what make us grow.

This isn't something that should stop when we grow older. Barbara Booth's great-great-grandmother was more than 100 years old when she pieced the three quilt tops that Barbara finished.

In fact, recent studies indicate that keeping your mind active is vitally important for the health of your brain. Learning new skills may play a role in countering the effects of Alzheimer's disease by building new pathways that bypass the plaques and tangles that clog and confuse an affected brain. You can think of right concentration as a brain exercise in which you strengthen your brain by encouraging it to build more of these pathways.

Right concentration also fosters a positive attitude. We can't, any of us, be happy and upbeat all the time, but a generally positive, hopeful outlook affects our physical as well as our mental health. We need to allow ourselves to be creative, whether it's expressed though quilt making or something else. This could, in fact, be our right purpose for quilting.

Once in a while, releasing our conscious worries and concentrating on our stitches, whether we're hand quilting, machine piecing, or any other phase of quilt making, frees the creative self to produce flashes of insight or self-awareness. These may be moments of problem solving as mentioned earlier, or they may be flashes of inspiration. I've caught myself thinking, "I'd never have thought of that!" when, of course, I just did. It seemed the thought simply came out of the blue.

When these things happen, we can appreciate them and be thankful for them, but we can't go into quilting expecting them. It's the effort to force an answer to a dilemma that blocks us from the insight and from creativity itself. It's only when we let all of it go that peace and occasionally insight comes.

Does this sound a little like prayer? Meditation and prayer are really just different approaches to the same thing. Of course, pastors and other religious leaders might not see it that way if you skip worship in favor of quilting. Think of quilting as a time for personal devotion, perhaps.

Perhaps that's why quilting circles lend themselves so well to church groups. Besides the fact that the quilts themselves are often given to charity, the activity of quilting can be a religious experience, as well.

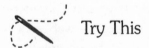 Try This

Quilt in a different location than you usually go to sew. Try a different room in your house that is perhaps quieter or has more sunshine. Colors can affect our moods, so the walls of the rooms may make concentration more or less difficult. Try taking a small project outside, perhaps to a park bench during your lunch break. Take a project with you to an appointment to see if your sewing will make an unpleasant setting more comfortable.

chapter nine

Follow
Your Bliss

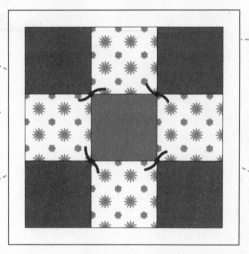

Tying Your Quilt

An alternative to actual quilting is to tie your quilt. This method is faster, and if you are using extra-thick batting, it is the only practical choice. Pin the layers together with large safety pins as you would if you were quilting. If you want to be sure your layers are smooth, thread baste as well. Determine an even placement of the ties. With a tapestry needle, run a strand of yarn or crochet cotton through the layers. Bring it back up again ¼ inch or so away. It's best to run the thread through the layers a second time and then tie the ends in a double knot. Keep a pair of needle-nose pliers handy to pull the needle through thick seam allowances.

This Is Mine

Quilting is a hobby, and as such, we ought to be able to do it our own way. We can do some research and listen to suggestions, but ultimately we need to do what's right for us. That isn't a difficult concept, but sometimes we're insecure enough that we have trouble doing it.

My daughter recalls bringing the 9-Patch blocks she had made for her first quilt into a fabric store to test them against fabric for her panels and borders. As the owner was ringing up her purchase, she asked Eden if she was going to hand stitch the quilt. Eden replied that she was planning on tying it, to which the owner responded, "You'll always regret it if you don't hand stitch it." Eden says she mumbled her excuses and felt foolish for each of them.

She went ahead and tied the quilt, although I think she had a few moments of uncertainty. Reminding herself that there would be other quilts helped. Also, she knew she wouldn't have time to hand quilt it and finishing the quilt quickly for a sense of accomplishment and for a pretty product were the important things at the moment. "Plus," she adds, "I like my little red knots."

I like the knots on my leafy quilt, too. I did them backward; that is, I used the front blocks to determine the even placement of the knots, but I brought the ends through to the back to tie them. The knots hardly show on the front, where the strips of the Roman Squares and large print blocks are going to dominate, anyway. On the back, the light tan ties match the binding and show up nicely against the white fabric that has a very faint leaf print. I have two completely different looks with one quilt, even though I tied it.

However, I really want to hand quilt the next one. They are different quilts with different purposes. And it's my hobby, so I get to do them my way. And so do the quilters who quilt without a hoop, in spite of it being technically "wrong" according to the experts. Even I caution against it in *The Everything® Quilting Book*. But every single change or addition in the evolution of quilt making resulted from someone doing things differently.

Barbara Booth's method of outlining her pictures through all the layers of her quilt is a new one to me. I'm not sure if you'd say she embroidered with quilting thread or quilted with an embroidery stitch, but you're not likely to run across it in any how-to book. The technique allowed her to show off her drawing in a way no standard technique could. And who knows, she or someone who sees her quilt may write about it in a quilting magazine and quilters all over the world will be "boothing" their quilts.

My boss, Irene Brown, and her mother, Arlene Couture, became the proud great-aunt and great-grandmother of a pair of twin girls a little ahead of schedule. They decided to make a couple of baby quilts over a weekend. They cut large butterflies out of leftover fabric, pinned them to the layered quilts, and machine appliquéd through all the layers, appliquéing and "quilting" at the same time. I thought the idea was so clever that I included it in *The Everything® Quilting Book*, but I'm sure a few perfectionists will frown on the concept.

But then, what would your great-grandmother, or even your mother for that matter, think of the new raw-edged quilts? Those are the new baby quilts in which double layers of flannel blocks are sewn together, leaving the raw edges to fray. It's not going to last, it doesn't look finished, the threads will plug up your washing machine are a few of the possible objections. But they are really cute and very popular. Someone had to do everything "wrong" to think of these quilts.

So, deciding to tie a quilt instead of quilting it seems like a pretty reasonable thing to do. When Joe's Grandma Benson tied her quilts, she always used wool yarn so it would shrink and tangle into little fuzzy buttons. She never had to worry about them coming untied. My daughter thought they looked like candy when she was little. She's not so fond of them now. But why did Grandma Benson always use wool? "Because you're supposed to." Forget that!

Sport yarn will thread through the eye of a smaller needle than regular 4-ply yarn, thus making it easier to pull though all the layers. I've used regular yarn, though, when I found the perfect color. I've tied with crochet cotton and once, on a pillow, I used embroidery floss. You'll have to ask me later how long it lasts. Or you can try it yourself and see.

That Wasn't Mine

I've taken the first several baby quilts I made out of storage just to look. Seeing my amateur stitches and my learn-as-you-go construction techniques brought bittersweet memories of that time in my life when I had little babies to care for.

I was also reminded of some earlier occasion when I had the quilts out and showed them to my elder son, Jon. He claimed he had never seen that first storybook quilt before. The third quilt, the one I had made for his younger brother, Paul, was a little familiar to him. I realized then that the biggest mistake I made with those baby quilts was not using them enough. If I had let Jon keep his quilt, drag it into the living room, take it along on car trips, and keep it at the foot of his bed even after his bed was bigger than the quilt, it would be familiar to him now. He would recognize it as part of his childhood. Memories would have added so much to the value of those first quilts.

But I didn't know that at the time. I wanted to pass the quilts on to my grandchildren, and I wanted them to be in good shape when I did. They are, in fact, almost like new.

When the kids wanted their quilts for their nests in front of the TV, I made them new, machine-made quilts. This set was more individualized. I knew the recipients then, as I hadn't when I made them their first ones.

Paul was probably three years old and interested in anything with wheels. The blocks on his quilt have appliquéd trucks, trains, and tractors. Eden, six, loved the Care Bears. Remember those short, fat, colorful bears with pictures on their tummies a couple of decades before Teletubbies? Each block of her quilt was a stuffed representation of those tummy pictures: a rainbow, smiling sun, heart, and so on. Eden wouldn't let me put that quilt away but kept it in her room in a basket with some pillows and a few stuffed animals that had been close friends in her childhood.

Nine-year-old Jon's favorite subject in school was science. Looking back, I'm sure this had more to do with his third-grade teacher's enthusiasm for class experiments (like "how long does it take a pumpkin to rot?") than it did with any natural tendencies, but that was what he loved at the time. His quilt has a microscope, volcano, bottles, beakers, batteries, and the Moon orbiting Earth. The quilt actually looks even more bizarre than it sounds, but he thought it was cool at the time.

I'm not sure when the quilt ceased to fit him. At some point it became clutter in his room, and I stored it away with the baby quilts. Of the two I made for Jon, the hand-quilted one with the cute hand-embroidered pictures and the machine-quilted one with the strange machine-appliquéd science pictures, guess which one means the most to Jon.

It's Your Thing

In the case of the quilts I made for my children, everyday use increased their value. In her short story *Everyday Use* (1973), Pulitzer Prize–winning author Alice Walker writes about a mother's decision of who will get two heirloom quilts. They had been promised to the shy daughter, Maggie, when she marries, but the elder daughter, Dee, who has moved to the city and made something of herself, wants them to hang on the wall.

When Dee suggests that Maggie would be "backward

enough" to use them and that they would be rags in five years, Mama says, "She can always make some more . . . Maggie knows how to quilt."

Because Mama's decision has more to do with what the girls need than with the quilts themselves, I'm glad to see Maggie get them. At the same time, I have some sympathy for Dee's point of view. The quilts were handmade by Dee's mother and grandmother from scraps of clothes worn by Dee's grandparents. There's even a piece from a great-grandfather's Civil War uniform. I would also have a desire to see the quilts preserved.

Pauline Palmer Meek is happy to admit she used the quilt her friend Geneva's mother made until it wore out, "frazzled beyond mending," as she puts it. The love it represented—of and for her lost friend and also for her own family—was more important than the relic itself.

Rick Cairn's decision is the opposite. He doesn't use his grandmother's quilt and is interested only in preserving (and treasuring) it. He wants to keep it as close as possible to the way it was when his grandmother and her quilting partners finished it.

Joe and I have tried to hit some kind of balance between these two views with his grandmother's quilt. It's folded over a quilt rack in our bedroom where we can see it every day. It gets used occasionally. While imbedded dirt will break down the fibers of any cloth, repeated washings wear out most quilts, so we don't use Grandma's quilt enough to necessitate much washing.

We're both happy with this arrangement for this quilt. It isn't quite relegated to everyday use, but it's still out where we can enjoy it. But this isn't going to work for everyone or with every quilt. There's no talking Rick into using his grandmother's quilt at all. And he's right. He knows what's right for him and that beautiful Improved 9-Patch quilt.

Most of the quilters I talked to say they store or display the old, inherited quilts, but expect the ones they make to be used. However, all those old quilts were new once, and the quilter expected *them* to be used.

Irene Brown has one quilt from each of her grandmothers. She knew these women, and she knows they made the quilts out of scraps because they felt guilty about wasting anything, and they would have considered storing these quilts an utter waste. Besides, she says, you're really warm when you have both "Grandmas" wrapped around you.

My sister Nancy recalls a wool quilt she thinks our mother, or possibly one of our grandmothers, made. It was a patchwork pieced probably from parts of old blankets and backed with flannel. Her main recollection was that she didn't want to touch the wool side. It was gone before I was ever aware of it. Nancy Collins remembers two quilts from her childhood that her mother made. She'd love to have one or the other of them, but they are gone. This is the price of using our quilts. Enjoying a quilt keeps those who come afterward from knowing it at all. The decision is very personal, and there will likely be regrets either way.

Quilts that are used, as I expect mine to be, show wear. Eventually they will get to a point where they are either mended or retired. There are two fates for "retired" quilts. They are either stored to stop the deterioration, or they are relegated to a status somewhat below everyday use. In the old days a quilt might be preserved between the layers of a new one. Today's high-quality battings are going to show off our handiwork so much better than a lumpy worn-out quilt. I can't imagine retiring a quilt that way now.

We have a second full-size quilt that may have been made by Grandma Benson. When Joe and I were married, it was already in the old bedding pile. The first time I saw it was when Joe got it out to cover some furniture we were moving. We used it a lot over the years as a picnic blanket and on the floor or yard when the kids were small. More recently, it's been used moving grown children and their stuff here and there. I never really looked at it until I got the quilting bug.

The colors are faded somewhat and there's a pink tinge around the edges that I think has been caused by the red of the blanket that was used as batting. The old blanket has torn away from the ties in places and is bunching in the corners. The binding and a few of the pieces are frayed.

But it's an interesting quilt to me. It's a 9-Patch like Grandma's other quilts, but four of the patches in each block are split 4-Patches in a Pinwheel design. There are panels between the blocks and at the intersection of these panels are small 4-Patches. This is a much more complicated design, using many more pieces, than the other two quilts, making me wonder if it might go back to an earlier generation.

Also of interest to me is the fact that the tiny triangles in the Pinwheels are hand pieced, but the larger pieces were sewn together with a machine. Did the quilter get started and change her mind? Were the tiny pieces difficult to guide through the machine? Or did one person start it and then pass it on to someone else to finish it?

Grandma Benson's mother died when she was small, so it is doubtful that she would have made the quilt. There were other sisters who would have inherited unfinished projects. But it might have come from some other relative.

My mother-in-law, Lucille Benson Detrixhe, doesn't recognize any of the fabric in the quilt. If her mother made it, she's sure it would have been very early in her life. This would make sense, since it was considered an old quilt as far back as Joe can remember.

So now I'm torn. In spite of its hard use, it is actually in pretty good shape. Do I preserve it for the tattered charm it holds for me—and apparently no one else? The story, the soul of the quilt, is gone or at least uncertain. Is it worth preserving? Do I send it on to use as furniture protector, picnic cloth, and other ignoble service? Is this use or abuse?

Or do I cut the ties off, rip out stitches that hold the binding, mend the few seams that are loose, replace a couple of frayed triangles with feed-sack fabric, and rebuild the quilt with new batting, backing, and ties? What would I do with it, then? The fabric will still be faded and thin. Do I repair it only to store it away? If we use a quilt until it's worn and then store it, we're storing a ratty-looking old quilt to pass on to someone who probably won't want it. Perhaps if we use a quilt to the point where it has lost its beauty, we might as well treat it as a rag.

I heard a story, secondhand, about a woman who saw her mother-in-law wipe down a newborn calf with an old quilt. The quilt was clearly worn-out, but it was just as clearly hand quilted. The younger woman was shocked. It colored her view of her mother-in-law.

Is this the price we pay for using these quilts? The old quilt had given the family years of pleasure before it came to this. Had it already "paid" for the hours it took to make it?

We each need to find where we draw the line, when we retire a quilt, when and if we store it away or consign it to "rag" use. And we need to respect the decisions our family makes as well.

A Balancing Act

Everything in our lives is a balancing act, though sometimes juggling seems to describe it better. As we've discussed, a hobby like quilting can give us balance. But it can also throw us out of balance. When does a hobby become an obsession? And would we recognize it when it did?

Several years ago, Joe belonged to a garden railroad club. He didn't feel as though we had much money to invest in his hobby, but he enjoyed owning a few cars and an engine or two. He also liked reading about what other enthusiasts were doing. That was why he joined the club and why he and I traveled to Topeka one Sunday afternoon to attend a gathering at club president Jerry Eaton's home.

We found the little house in an older neighborhood and were shown around to the backyard. Half a dozen other couples were enjoying soft drinks and snacks. The entire backyard was dominated by the host's railroad. The patio with a small raised deck was integrated into the layout with the tracks going under the deck at one point. I think Joe was a little overwhelmed by the amount of planning, landscaping, and *work* the whole thing must have taken, to say nothing of the constant maintenance.

Meanwhile, Jerry's wife, Marge, took the ladies inside to show us her sewing room. The way her husband was involved in his garden railroad, she was involved in quilting. I remember being impressed with the storage designed for her fabric and with the fact that her fabric was all sorted by color. The closet had shelves for boxes of smaller scraps. Shelves over her sewing machine were full of sewing notions; more shelves held her books and magazines. She had lots of three-drawer plastic boxes for keeping her quilting supplies and materials for her other hobbies sorted.

On that Sunday afternoon, she told us she had lots of quilts in progress at any given time. I remember thinking, "Why?" It seemed she ought to finish one once in a while. I wasn't into quilting at the time, obviously.

A couple of other women were also quilters and they talked quilts for a time. I was pretty much excluded from the conversation. I had made the baby quilts and was working on a Cathedral Window quilt off and on (three years off, three months on). I was wearing a sweater I had made, but that counted for nothing with these women.

I remember Joe and I wondering if this woman and her husband might have too much free time. Their hobbies, it seemed to us, had become obsessions. However, they were both retired. They had had their years of balancing careers and hobbies. What was wrong with finally getting to do what they wanted to do? Perhaps Joe and I were a little jealous.

In a recent conversation, I asked Marge how many projects she has going. She told me sixty-seven. Surely she had said six or seven, I thought later. I called her back to clarify. No, I had heard her right. Sixty-seven was the number the last time she bothered to count, but that included all projects, needlepoint and other handwork as well as quilts. "Only about forty are quilts," she says.

I find that I need my creative hobbies more as my life becomes more stressful, just when I have less time for them. I actually have five quilts going right now. The Take Along quilt travels so well, I never work on it at home. The ongoing Cathedral Window quilt was stalled while I waited for some of it to be returned after being photographed for *The Everything®️ Quilting Book*. (A likely excuse, you say.)

A third quilt, the one I cut out at the retreat, is on hold until I get time to do some hand appliqué. The fourth is the Zen quilt. Since it will consist mainly of blocks I've made for the illustrations in this book, it will be set aside once I send those blocks to my editor. It was my top priority until I got those illustration blocks finished.

The last quilt is one I suddenly decided I had to make first. It's the sunflower quilt for Paul's bed. It's the current priority for the sewing room.

Of course, I have all the fabric I need for two more quilts and most of the fabric for two others. I tell myself not to start them until I finish one of the others (or at least the sweater I'm knitting, which is my current priority for the living room). Somehow, five quilts in progress is acceptable while six seems to be too many. Perhaps this is only because five is the most I've had going at one time. Perhaps, if I had some reason to start a sixth, that would become my new limit. Someone else visiting my sewing room might well say I'm obsessed. I think I'm just having fun.

What difference does it make if I work a little on one, then a little on another. Sometimes I want to appliqué. Sometimes I want to hand quilt. Sometimes I want to sew things on my machine. And sometimes, what I really want to do is plan something new. None of my quilts really *need* to be finished.

Marge says she prefers "passion" to obsession. She says if you set a quilt aside long enough, it's like starting a new quilt when you get it out again. Several other quilters say they have quilts they've started and set aside. The fact only bothers those patch-by-patch quilters.

Catherine Silhan admits she becomes momentarily obsessed with her hobby. At times she'll put off work because she's totally into her quilting. Sharon Fields says she's allowed to be obsessed, because she's a quilting instructor. Nancy Chaffee Parker has also taught quilting and led retreats. She says it's just a hobby, but she loves getting other people excited about quilting. I suppose that makes her a carrier.

Nancy Collins assures me she isn't obsessed with quilting.

It's the whole sewing thing that obsesses her. I remember her mentioning, before she retired, that she'd get grumpy if she had to go too long without sewing. Lately she's been making up for lost time. She pressures herself to finish one project before starting another by telling herself *this* is the project that matches the thread in the sewing machine.

I think our hobbies truly become obsessions when we use them to hide from something else in our lives. A friend told me about her sister—I'll call her Vera—who quilts. Vera loves to quilt, her sister says, because she hates her job. She makes it through a day at work because she knows she will be attending a quilter's guild meeting or teaching a quilting class that evening. She makes it through a week of work by knowing she can quilt all weekend.

I'm not sure how much time this leaves Vera for her family or other aspects of her life. It may not be as bad as her sister describes, but if it's true at all, Vera's life is out of balance. It seems we should know if our lives are out of harmony, as the Native Americans say. Perhaps we do, but we can't always figure out exactly what is wrong, or if we can, we don't always know what to do about it. Escape is easier.

Do What Ya Wanna Do

When the late Joseph Campbell, foremost interpreter of myth, said, "Follow your bliss," he was speaking of our vocation. He said we ought to find a way to make a living doing what we love. That's a wonderful notion, but how many of us manage it?

Most of us work the job we can get, earn enough money to support ourselves in some style or other, put a little away if we're lucky, and spend some on what we enjoy. The best most of us hope for is to find some pleasure in our job.

Don't misunderstand me. I consider working at home, raising children, and making a home a worthy vocation. Some women who work outside the home wish they didn't, while some who are at home feel guilty about not being employed. These, too, are things you need to consider if you're going to come close to following your bliss.

For a few years, I was able to follow Joseph Campbell's advice. I called myself a full-time novelist. During that time, I did less sewing, knitting, and crocheting. In fact, if I started any handwork project, my son Jon, a writer himself, would ask if the writing was going badly. It usually was.

Losing my publisher threw me into the ranks of the unemployed. While my agent worked to find me a publisher, I had to find a job that had nothing to do with the things I loved. I did apply at a fabric store, but they weren't hiring.

I enjoy the job I have now as secretary for Irene's accounting business and her husband's plumbing and electric business. I feel confident that I can do the work, and more important, I like the people I work with. Besides I'm also a writer again, even though it isn't fiction. I still dream of writing novels, of following my bliss, but things are balanced for me about as well as they can be right now.

However, for a few months, I worked at a job I hated.

Never mind all my reasons for hating it; it sapped my spirit so entirely that I had trouble even enjoying my hours off. Perhaps if I had stayed there longer, I would have developed effective ways to put it aside and concentrate on my creative activities when I had the chance. I certainly didn't have any luck writing while I was working there.

The pay at that job was an insult, but I doubt if any amount of money would have made it worth staying. I feel for Vera and wonder if she's truly making enough money to make the job worth doing day after miserable day.

Of course, it's also possible that it isn't the job itself that Vera hates, but that it's anything that isn't quilting. But whether that makes quilting an obsession for her or just truly her bliss is not for me to judge.

It would be wonderful if Vera could make a living quilting. She can probably make a little with the quilting classes. She might find an outlet to sell her quilts, but unless she could get her fabric wholesale, she won't get much more than the money she spent on her materials. So a job that allows her time and energy to quilt may be her best bet.

Kathryne Perney owns the Quilting Station, where she quilts for other people on her quilting machine. A couple of other quilters I talked to have done some hand quilting for other people, but neither felt they could really charge enough to compensate for their time. Everyone else seemed happy to keep quilting a hobby.

I don't believe we should stay in jobs we hate. One of the

Buddhist keys to happiness is right livelihood. Ancient as this list is, it shows some recognition that what we do to earn a living affects our spirits. Meditating about our job while we quilt can help us see if we are hiding in our hobby or using our hobby to balance our job.

So how do you keep quilting a hobby when other people try to turn it into a job? Bonnie pleads lack of time when someone asks her to make a quilt. Marge Eaton said yes and it took ten years. Eden suggests you say, "You can't afford me."

But what if they could? Would you make a quilt for someone else if you could name your price? Would that make it any less a hobby? On the other hand, most quilters love to *give* their quilts away.

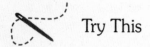 Try This

Plan a quilt with blocks that represent different aspects of your work. Consider the separate tasks you do. Consider the people you work with. You don't have to get terribly elaborate; abstract images may describe your coworkers or clients or their duties. This is an exercise in self-discovery. If you don't work outside the home, use the household tasks or your volunteer work. Staying home isn't old-fashioned, but you might want to revert to old-fashioned images of what you actually do: a washboard, a treadle sewing machine, and so on. This can be done with some traditional jobs, as well. Sketch out some original blocks, but also consider the names of old standards. Does your design make you happy? Maybe you want to go ahead and make the quilt.

If the pattern called Devil's Claw is the one you chose to represent your boss, and you want to do the whole quilt in shades of gray, perhaps you need to look at making some changes in your vocation.

chapter ten

All Things
Must Pass

Binding Your Quilt

The last step in quilt construction is binding the edges. Cut strips of cloth 2 inches wide and sew them together end to end. Press the raw edges of your binding strip under a scant ½ inch. Line up the raw edge of the strip with the raw edge of the quilt, and stitch along the fold line. Turn the binding to the other side, and machine stitch close to the turned-under edge, or hemstitch the binding down by hand. The only hard part is how to handle the corners. There are several tricks to making square or mitered corners, but the easiest thing to do is to round off the corners of your quilt and ease a little extra binding under the needle as you stitch around the curve.

Project to Product

Marge Eaton shared a toast she'd heard at a quilting retreat. "Here's to fun, friends, fabric . . . and finishing."

Several quilters cited finishing as their favorite part of quilt making. Several mentioned loving the feeling of accomplishment. A few, like Eden, felt empowered by seeing their first quilt completed. It meant they could move on to more challenging projects.

For others, finishing was important because of how the quilt would be used. Clara MacDougall says she likes to finish so she can give the quilt away. She actually only gives away about half the quilts she makes, but those are the ones she's most willing to talk about.

Mary Ellen Giglio says finishing is her favorite part, too. She feels as though she's really accomplished something. Similarly, Bonnie may express what a lot of quilters feel when she says that at work she does the same thing day after day, never really finishing anything. It's the same at home with the housework. You can clean today, but your house will be dirty again in a few days, and cooking and washing dishes seem like never-ending tasks. When Bonnie finished her first quilt, she nearly cried. It felt great to be so proud of something she had done, something she had started and taken step by step to the end.

Marsha Wentz says her favorite part is finishing; she says she works best with a deadline. Without a particular finishing day to work toward, such as a visit across the country to a child's home, quilt tops tend to pile up, waiting for her to quilt them. Though she loves to quilt, she likes the faster gratification of piecing; she feels a little reluctance about finishing a project. "Once you've sewn on the label," she says, "it's out there for others to criticize."

I don't think I worry about criticism, but I tend to postpone binding my quilts. I leave my otherwise finished quilts in my sewing room, sometimes for weeks, as if they need to cure like meat or age like wine. I fold them carefully and marvel at how great they look . . . except for that raw edge and those little tufts of batting hanging out here and there.

On the one hand, binding can be difficult, especially if you've left problems from previous steps as I did with the uneven layers of my leafy quilt. But even so, binding can be done in an afternoon if you do it all on the sewing machine. Add an additional evening or two to hand stitch, and it's still not that big a task. While pressing under the edges on a strip more than 7 yards long can be tedious, there are plenty of other steps in quilt construction just as repetitive.

On the other hand, I just seem to be reluctant to perform that last step. It's different if I have a deadline. If the quilt is a gift and there's a specific event I want it finished for, I'll get it done on time, though I may still wait for the last possible minute to do that binding.

All in all, I suspect my procrastination has little to do with the actual act of binding itself.

Twenty years ago we had a rather eccentric neighbor who never seemed to finish any of the many projects she started. When I visited her, she liked to show me the curtains she was

making, the chair cushions she was needlepointing, the furniture she was refinishing, all for the odd little house where she
lived all alone. I don't remember her ever showing me things
she had finished, and I know I saw those same unfinished curtains spread across the bed in her spare bedroom at least four
times, though eventually they were nearly hidden by another
sewing project she had piled on top of them.

My husband and I used to joke that she thought she would
live forever if she never finished anything, that God wouldn't
take her with so much left undone. It makes me think of old
Mrs. Remington, the widow of the rifle manufacturer, who
believed she would live as long as she kept adding on to her
house. The Winchester Mystery House, with its stairs that lead
nowhere and rooms with no purpose, is now a tourist attraction
in San Jose, California. Of course it didn't work for either of
them. My neighbor eventually moved to a rest home and died
when she was in her seventies.

Now that I'm a little closer to the age she was when she
lived nearby, I understand a couple of things I didn't then. The
projects she was working on were the ones that excited her. She
didn't get quite the same kick out of showing off something that
was finished. When the curtains no longer excited her, she left
them while she worked on other things.

If you came to my house, today, I'd show you my five
quilts-in-progress. If you noticed the Watercolor quilt on my
living room wall, I'd tell you about it, too, of course, but it's not
as fun to talk about as the ones that only exist in their entirety in
my head.

Also, I'm more tolerant of the idea of having several projects going at once than I was back then. At the time, I always
had a child three or under and a small house. Projects not only
had to be packed away to protect little fingers from scissors and
pins and to protect the projects from unauthorized alterations,
but it all had to be stored away in fairly limited space. There
had to be a limit, too, on the number of projects I allowed
myself to start before something got finished.

Nowadays I could probably rival my former neighbor with
my list of ongoing projects, though Marge Eaton, with her forty
quilts, would still beat me in any works-in-progress contest.
They are easy for me to justify, at least to myself. Having quilts
in different phases gives me very different tasks for different
times. If I want to sit quietly and watch TV, listen to music, or
meditate, there is always some kind of handwork waiting for
me, whether it's quilting, piecing, or blocks that need embroidery or appliqué. If I'm wound up from work and can't sit still,
some energetic cutting and machine piecing always help me
unwind.

All these projects are like friends I turn to—until it's time to
bind them. Then I let them sit. I don't believe I'll get a reprieve
from the Grim Reaper because I've started so many projects. In
some cases, I may have lost my enthusiasm for the project, like
the Cathedral Window quilt. Twenty-some years on one quilt is
worse than my neighbor's curtains. However, I think in most
cases, I'm simply reluctant to see them move from project to
product. When I finally decide to bind one of these waiting
quilts, it's usually out of a desire to return to a project that I've

started to miss. Picking it up is bittersweet because I know I only get to have one last afternoon with it before it's over.

Nothing Stays the Same but Change

Change is inevitable. From new fabric to scattered pieces to a quilt on the bed, our quilts tend to chart the passage of time. All the quilts I've made represent a period in my life that is gone. Looking at the differences between the quilts I'm making now and the ones I made twenty-five years ago brings this home to me.

As I worked on the blocks to illustrate the beginning of the chapters of this book, I realized that there won't be enough blocks to make a whole quilt. I've decided to add a block for each of my children to represent what they have been up to during the time I've spent writing about quilting. My eldest, Jon, filmed a feature-length movie in our community last summer. I alternately pieced on a Dresden Plate and edited chapters of *The Everything® Quilting Book* while I guarded camera batteries he was recharging at a city park during one day of filming. This movie about militant separatists and heroic Girl Scouts serves as his master's thesis at New York University's film school. I'm not sure what I'll do to represent this movie on a quilt block, but I'm sure he'll have some offbeat suggestions for me.

Eden earned her master's in political science from the University of Michigan. She also learned to quilt. I think I'll try to appliqué the burning lamp, which is a symbol on the university's seal and a fairly common symbol of higher learning. But somewhere on her block, I want to put a tiny 9-Patch made from scraps left from her first quilt.

Paul's National Guard unit was called to active duty, and he is with Task Force Eagle in Bosnia. I'm going to try to represent the army's eagle symbol on a block. He earned his wings more than a year ago, but I'll probably include them somewhere, too, because I'm still in awe of the fact that my little boy can fly.

These three blocks are a far cry from the cars, Care Bears, and chemistry symbols in the quilts I made my kids twenty-five years ago, even though there was an airplane and a helicopter on Paul's old quilt. So much has changed in their lives and mine that it seems as though we were all different people then.

What Goes Around Comes Around

In another sense, the more things change, the more they stay the same. Barbara Booth shared the following about the three quilt tops she inherited: Her great-great-grandmother Ruth came back to Middle Creek in Marion County, Kansas, when she was one hundred. She was returning to her old home where her son John, a Civil War veteran and elderly himself at this point, lived with his unmarried daughter Clara. Clara had to find something to keep Ruth busy and set her to work making quilt tops from cloth in the scrap basket. Barbara inherited three of an unknown number of quilt tops that Ruth pieced together during the last seven years of her life.

In an oddly reversed sort of way, this mirrors Marguerite Martin's story of her Lone Star quilt, a task given to her by a caregiver to keep her busy when she was a girl. Together they illustrate the cycle of life.

Becky Fooshee Walters writes that her mother, Fern Fooshee, frequently asked her own mother, Hattie Ingeroll, why she spent so many hours quilting. Between quilts she made for herself and family, Hattie often quilted for other people for very little pay. Though Becky doesn't remember Hattie ever giving any real answer, Fern had a quilt in Hattie's frame shortly after Hattie died. Had Fern really been baffled by her mother's love of quilting or was she hoping her mother could explain her own pull to the frame?

When my daughter uses Kevin's grandmother's old sewing machine, she wonders how much Vi used it raising two kids and making gifts for four grandchildren. Was sewing a pleasure or a burden? Was the machine usually folded up inside its wooden cabinet or out ready to use? When Eden finished the quilt, she took pictures and sent them to Vi in the nursing home, wanting to let the old woman know she appreciated the gift of the sewing machine and was putting it to good use.

With my daughter quilting now, I feel a generational connection to the future through quilting. Other than my respect for the old craft and craftswomen, I don't really have a connection to the past. My grandmothers were both gone before I was born. If they quilted, none of their work survived to my generation. I didn't even know about the wool quilt my mother might have made until my sister Nancy told me about it.

But for several quilters and nonquilters who wrote me, the memories of Grandma at the quilt frame help to define these women for them. For example, Becky Fooshee Walters remembers her grandmother wouldn't quilt on Sunday, but other times she might sing her "church songs" while she quilted. Young Becky didn't think her grandmother could carry a tune. She doesn't remember her grandmother ever saying if she liked to quilt; it was just what Grandma did.

Our ancestors are a deeper part of us than we realize sometimes. This is true of the ones who touch our lives on a daily basis and the ones who we remember, but also of the ones deeper in our families' past. Their beliefs, their ways, and sometimes even their tastes influence us whether we're aware of it or not. Often the first quilts mentioned during my interviews were the quilts that were made by mothers, grandmothers, and other women even farther down the family tree. I don't believe it's simply those quilts' age that make people cherish them. There's more to them than their antique value.

Kathryne Perney has her great-great-grandmother's quilt, which was made in the 1860s or 1870s. Marsha Wentz has a quilt her mother made, although her mother didn't quilt within Marsha's memory. She also has one her grandmother pieced and hired quilted. These two are extra-special because they were on Marsha's bed when she was a child, reminding her of her own past as well as the women who made the quilts. Sharon Fields used to have a quilt her husband's great-grandmother had made. She passed it on to her daughter who had a place to display it. Lillian Ruud has the Friendship quilt made for her husband's grandmother in 1896. These family heir-looms are all links to the unique women who made them.

Not one of these heirs or the others I talked to discussed the physical condition of the quilts or their possible commercial value. These things were totally beside the point. The value of these quilts goes much deeper than what the rest of us would see. Whether these ancestors ever knew the current owner, their heirs feel as if they know the quilter through the quilts. The only ones who mentioned the quilter's skill were the ones who considered her exceptionally good. One mentioned that the flowers on the quilts let her know that the quilter loved to garden. I know my husband's grandmother was frugal from her scrap quilts, but I also know she was generous since the quilts were gifts.

The quilts, like Barbara Booth's, that cross generational lines seem to give their owners a special pleasure. Besides having one or two quilts her great-great-grandmother made, Catherine Silhan has one her grandmother made the blocks for, Catherine pieced together, and her mother quilted. Becky Fooshee Walters has a quilt her mother and grandmother pieced together and her grandmother quilted. These quilts hold the spirits of not one but two or three women. They illustrate how our own stories are entwined with our ancestors. These women—Barbara, Catherine, and Becky—are each proud to be part of a multigenerational work of art.

Becky remembers helping her grandmother quilt when she was about nine or ten. She never stayed with it very long before moving on to other activities, but she knew she quilted just as well as her grandmother. She knew this because when she'd go back and look for her stitches the next day, she couldn't tell them from any of the other stitches on the quilt. It wasn't until years later that she learned Grandma would stay up late after Becky was asleep and take out all her awkward stitches and replace them with her own tiny, professional stitches. Grandma's conduct is impressive. She never belittled Becky's efforts but welcomed her company and "help" again and again.

Rick Cairns remembers taking a few stitches on his grandmother's quilt as well. He never mentioned the possibility of her taking them back out, and she might not have.

I remember when I was in my teens, my parents took care of one of my nephews one evening. Sometime during the toddler's stay, my dad showed him his reflection in the bathroom mirror. The boy reached out and leaned against the glass, leaving a perfect tiny handprint. After he went home, my parents had quite a discussion on whether they should clean the mirror ever again. I can't remember who took which side, but I know they would have been in agreement if *I* had been the one to make the print. I also know who would have had to clean it off.

But grandchildren are special. Rick's grandmother may have treasured those few stitches of his the same way he treasures her quilt.

As we get older, we understand better how relationships change. When we're young, we think that the way things are is how things have always been and always will be. Grandma has always been an old lady, has always quilted, and will always be there. She may let me take a few stitches on the quilt until something more interesting distracts me and I run off to another activity. But I can always come back and stitch again.

When we are young adults, we know that things will change. Our children will outgrow their baby quilts, and their children will outgrow theirs. But we don't fully understand how quickly those changes take place. We know, but we don't understand.

Maybe we never can understand exactly, but as we get older, we try. Right understanding is the eighth and final Zen key to happiness and perhaps the one that is the most elusive. We come to understand one change in our lives only to have something else change on us. Eventually we piece a quilt that a daughter, or a sister-in-law, or a great-great-granddaughter finishes for us.

Not to get too maudlin here, but our time is limited. We realize this when we treasure an antique quilt and think about the life of the one who made it. She had her dreams and disappointments. She could not have imagined us, though she may have tried. Chances are some descendant of ours will hold our quilts and wonder about us.

When we store away a baby quilt and when we get it out again for another generation, we have to realize how quickly time has flown. We remember choosing this fabric, taking those stitches.

As we teach the next generation how to quilt, there's a realization that our role has shifted. With Zen, our job is to find our purpose in each new phase as it comes.

The Family That Quilts Together

A common hobby can help bring families together. It can create an excuse for us to get together, as the quilting class did for Mary Ellen Giglio and her sisters. It can give us a common purpose, as Sister Betty Suther's annual quilting weekend with her family.

It gives us a common language and alertness when we seek out particular aspects of our hobby to share, such as fabric, patterns, and quilting stories we know the other quilters will appreciate.

Teresa LaFlair has quilted with four of her sisters in class and occasionally on a Saturday. She wants to get them all together to make a pattern she found called Seven Sisters. There are two sisters who don't quilt, but I think Teresa should find some way to get them involved in the enterprise as well.

Sometimes these familial connections are cut short much too soon. Florence Baker and her identical twin sister, Florine, made six quilts together. Tragically, Florine died in 1947 and a lot of the fun went out of quilting for Florence. She made a few on her own and did some quilting for other people, but she never threw her heart into it again.

Other times, the connections spring up unexpectedly. Though her mother sewed, Cindy Kahrs didn't have any generational connections to quilting when she started. She does now. All three of her daughters quilt. Her youngest, Kelsey, just completed her third quilt, a doll quilt, which she made all by herself except for the binding. She's been quilting now for two years, having started at age eight. "Quilting is more than a hobby to me," Cindy writes. "It has kept me close to my daughters. We share e-mails and books about quilting and keep each other inspired.

"Someday soon," Cindy adds, "I am going to surprise my mom with a quilt. Had she not given me that fabric over twenty-seven years ago, I may never have started to quilt at all."

Now, my daughter and I often share our latest quilting and sewing plans and adventures when we talk by phone or e-mail. We had a similar connection with other handiwork over the years. When she was still home and even while she was in college, we would spend a weekend afternoon with our handwork, she knitting or cross stitching perhaps while I crocheted or quilted. We'd talk and laugh, share ideas, and stitch away. It's much harder to find those afternoons now, but we manage once in a while.

Quilting has become more special to me since she joined me in the activity. It's not just because it's great having someone to trade fabrics and patterns with or to bounce ideas off. I could find another quilter for those things. And I could find another quilter to accompany me on fabric store shopping sprees or quilting retreats. But doing these things with my daughter brings us a little closer together. Also, I quilt now knowing someone will come after me who appreciates what goes into a quilt because she's made some herself.

I can look at her talent with a needle and think she's inherited that from me. I also remember that her great-grandmother Benson with her thrifty 9-Patch quilts has passed her genes to

Eden as well. When our color preferences differ, which they often do, I wonder if it's the time or her youth or if I raised her to be bolder than I allow myself to be. Then I wonder if I should try a little more of that.

R-E-S-P-E-C-T

Because of the love, the historical and familial connections, and all the other spiritual aspects of quilt making, the quilts mean much more to most of us than the blankets, and even the works of art, that they are. My interest in history, especially the settlement of the American West, my love of handcrafts and sewing, my fascination with puzzles and geometry probably all contribute to my love of quilts and quilting. I know from my interviews that other people share that love, but for different reasons.

Unfortunately, once in a while, someone misses the point entirely. Eden visited a Kansas University art museum when it was featuring a showing of antique Amish quilts. She describes it as a beautiful, uplifting exhibit. She studied each quilt carefully and read each description. It seems the descriptions delved into the piecing designs, fabrics, and colors and virtually ignored the actual quilting stitches.

Amish quilting traditions involve some pretty elaborate stitching, and Eden would have liked to have learned the names of the different quilting designs or at least to have had these time-consuming stitches acknowledged.

Before she left the museum, Eden made an entry in the guest book to mention the omission. Then she leafed back through the pages to see what other visitors had written. She found this across from a man's name: "These belong on the back of a couch, not in a museum."

Clearly, someone had dragged the man to the exhibit. I don't know whom I feel the most sorry for, the quilt lover who had to suffer his presence while she tried to enjoy the exhibit, or the man who was led to water, so to speak, and refused to admit he was thirsty.

Of course, those quilts deserved to be honored in a museum exhibit. Their age alone would qualify them. The staples of any antique museum are utilitarian objects from an earlier time. Would he have been more impressed with old china and a butter churn? Maybe.

But the quilts are also works of art, soft sculpture, if you must have artistic terms, a study in color and texture done in stitches instead of strokes.

But you already understand that or you wouldn't have read this far. What would we have to do to convince this unbeliever? And what brought him to this sad pass in the first place? Did his grandmother slap his hand and chase him away from the quilt frame? We'll never know, but we may run into people like him. I suppose compassion and Zen are our best responses.

Actually quilts are even more than wo... of art, connections to individual family members, creative outlets, and symbols of loving relationships. They are part of our cultural conscious...

As such, they symbolize the very concepts of home and family, love and more.

For instance, I watched a romantic comedy recently that I had seen before. Unlike my previous viewing in which I was focused on the story, this time I noticed details and saw a quilt that I had overlooked before. To draw a contrast between one woman who was married with two children, and her boyfriend-hopping friend, the moviemakers had put a Double Wedding Ring quilt on the married woman's bed. We see this near the beginning of the movie, when she and her family, including a dog, are all interacting one Saturday morning. The quilt reinforces the picture of the happy family.

In the future, pay a little attention to the background of movies and television shows. Notice when quilts are used to define a character or family, from the names and symbolism of the quilt patterns to the quilt's everyday use or its preservation on the wall. See whether you agree with the appropriateness of a particular quilt.

And then be alert to the quilts in the background of your life. Do they decorate and enrich your life the way you want them to? Maybe one of those quilts stored in the trunk *should* be on the back of your couch. Do your speech and conduct show you to be the beautiful person you want reflected in your quilts? Are you putting the right effort into the right purpose? Concentrate for a moment on your life as you're living it today. Is quilting in balance with work and love and faith? If not, meditate on what seems wrong and see if there aren't solutions waiting for you to recognize them.

Living My "Quilt" Zen

I want to surround myself with quilts and mark the seasons with quilt-related activities. First, spring is the time for new beginnings. I want to plan new projects inspired by the rebirth of nature. My crocuses bloom, sometimes through the snow on a sunny day in late February. By the time the daffodils and tulips open, the misguided fruit trees have probably already blossomed and frozen. In the spring, I think of cleaning and brightening and decorating my home. I want to make a wall hanging to welcome spring and table runners to welcome guests. I think of digging out quilted crafts that have been stored away in dark attics or trunks and bringing them into my sunny home.

I want to translate spring housecleaning into organizing my sewing room, sorting my fabric, and maybe even servicing my sewing machine. When the iris by my doorstep blooms, it's truly spring and the easiest time to start something new, to pull out that reserved fabric and make those first cuts that commit it to a particular quilt. I'm braver in the spring.

For me, summer is for sewing. I may have less time for it when faced with other activities including gardens with tomatoes and corn and raspberries if we're lucky, but I have more energy, too. Those pieces ready at my sewing machine or in the basket in the living room will call to me once in a while. I like to hand piece in the summer, especially if I can work in small sections so there's nothing warm on my lap.

And even if there isn't much time to sew, there are flowers and sunshine to encourage me, family gatherings to challenge me, and vacations with new settings and new fabric stores to inspire me. And those piecing and appliqué projects can travel right along with me.

Autumn makes me want to lay in warm blankets for winter, even if I don't really need them. Tying extra-thick quilts seems like a good idea. Or maybe this fall I ought to pull out that box of wool fabric just to see if it would be fun to work with.

Some people may think of fall as the beginning of the end and dread the shorter days and the loss of all the green in the landscape. But I've always felt most creative in the fall as milo turns auburn and the scorching days come to an end. Ideas for new novels always come easiest then. I don't know if it's the warm colors with the leaves themselves seeming to burst into bloom, or if it's the transition from a hectic summer to a quieter winter to come.

When I had school-age kids, I felt as though my time was my own again as they returned to a school schedule. Projects could progress more quickly. I have a little of the same sense now, even though the kids have all left the nest. Not all their stuff has, but they have.

Winter is the time to settle in and quilt. Even with my hoop, there's a lot of quilt left to hang on my lap, but I welcome it in the wintertime. I set up the hoop near the living room fireplace. Kansas winters are a mix of ice storms and mild sunny days, and I can sew and reflect on the extremes of weather and life and the contrasts of color on my quilt.

I rush to finish projects as the winter holidays bring a new round of gatherings and celebrations with gift giving and decorating. At the same time, I feel more settled in the winter and can spend longer periods sitting still without feeling restless.

Of course, most of us lead rather hectic lives all year-round. Those quiet moments to sew come whenever we can find the time. Or whenever we can make them. Yet the changes in the seasons do affect our activities and our thinking as well. Understanding and appreciating the changing seasons and how we change with them help us accept the bigger changes that are part of life.

Wherever you find yourself on life's journey, may your mistakes be easily ripped out and repaired, may your family and friends blanket you with love, and may your path be as straight as Grandma's stitches.

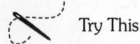 Try This

Visit a quilt museum or quilt show. As you walk among the many beautiful quilts, try to look at them as one artist would look at another artist's work. Let the quilts inspire you. Try to find a new appreciation of what each quilt represents in time and creativity. If the quilts are antiques, consider the differences in the world at the time the quilts were made. At the same time, consider the things that were the same.

appendix a

9-Patch
for Beginners

The 9-Patch quilt is the perfect quilt for beginners. You'll get lots of practice cutting and sewing without the extra problems involved with triangles or odd-shaped pieces. These instructions are for a double bed–size quilt. I like a lot of overhang on my quilts so I usually need a size larger package of batting. The finished measurements for this quilt are approximately 101 × 83 inches, which allows for about 14 inches of overhang on the sides and at the foot and approximately the same extra inches to tuck under and extend over the pillows at the head.

The quilt will consist of twenty 15-inch blocks arranged in five rows of four. The blocks are separated by 3-inch panels and surrounded by 7-inch borders.

Fabrics

If you are a beginner, you probably don't have a stash of fabric, yet. This pattern is designed with you in mind and calls for purchasing three coordinating fabrics. I recommend cotton, perhaps two fabrics with similar but different size motifs and a third fabric of a solid or tone-on-tone print that picks up your favorite color in the prints. Avoid one-way prints—that is, prints that must be turned in one direction to look right-side up.

Two fabrics will be used for the alternating squares in the 9-Patch blocks. The third fabric, the border fabric, will be used for the panels between the blocks and for the center square of each of the 9-Patch blocks. You will need:

4 yards of border fabric
2 yards each of two coordinating fabrics
3 yards of extra-wide backing fabric or 6 yards of regular 42-inch or 44-inch fabric
One package of polyester batting (check dimensions on the package)
Approximately 10$\frac{1}{3}$ yards of doublewide bias binding tape (optional)
One large or two small spools of thread for piecing
Sports-weight yarn and a sharp tapestry needle for tying

Cutting the Border Fabric

Prepare your new fabric, including your backing, as described at the beginning of Chapter 1. From your border fabric, you will need:

4 horizontal panels, $3\frac{1}{2} \times 69\frac{1}{2}$ inches
15 vertical panels, $3\frac{1}{2} \times 15\frac{1}{2}$ inches
2 side borders, $7\frac{1}{4} \times 87\frac{1}{2}$ inches
2 end (top and bottom) borders, $7\frac{1}{4} \times 83$ inches
20 squares, $5\frac{1}{2} \times 5\frac{1}{2}$ inches

Figuring out how to cut all the necessary pieces out of a minimum of fabric with little or no internal piecing requires the use of some applied geometry. But remember, you will lose an inch or two when you trim the raw edges at the ends of your fabric. There could easily be a small amount of shrinkage, and the clerk might not have been perfectly accurate. While you should be able to cut the pieces listed from $3\frac{2}{3}$ yards, if that is all you bought, it is unlikely you will actually have that much fabric when you start to cut. Also, some of the longer pieces will have to be pieced. That's why I recommend 4 yards, even though there will be some left over.

Trim both ends of the fabric. The following steps assume you have about 4 inches less than the full 4 yards of fabric or 140 inches of fabric that is at least 41 inches wide. The steps may seem somewhat complicated to figure out on your own. Don't worry. A sketch can sometimes help you decide how to approach the task. Most patterns will call for plenty of fabric, so several different approaches will work. I like to make a game out of trying to have my leftovers come out, as nearly as possible, to one large piece instead of several little ones—that's what you'll have when you're done if you follow my instructions.

Step One: Horizontal Panels

Begin by trimming away the selvage along one side. Parallel to this trimmed edge, cut two strips, 3½ inches wide down the full 4 yards. Pulling a thread as a guide is probably the easiest way to do this. Each of these strips is a little more than you will need for two horizontal panels. You can cut them in half or leave them as they are.

Fold the strips together and set them aside. Pinning a scrap of paper to your pieces with their future use written on it will help you keep them straight.

Step Two: Vertical Panels

Cut one more 3½-inch-wide strip down the length of the fabric. This piece will be used for nine of the 15½-inch-long vertical panels. No need to cut it to the proper lengths. Set this piece aside. You will cut the remaining six panels later.

Step Three: Borders

Measure 87½ to 88 inches off one end of your piece. Set the remaining approximately 52 inches aside. Cut the larger piece into four long strips, each 7¼ inches wide. You probably won't have much more than the selvage left. These four strips will be the border pieces. They will be trimmed to the correct length later. Label them and set them aside.

Remaining Horizontal Panels

From the approximately 52 × 30-inch piece of fabric you have left, cut two 3½-inch strips the long way. Each of these strips will yield three more horizontal panels. Fold them with the long piece that was set aside and label them.

Center Patches

You will need twenty center patches, which will be cut from the rest of the fabric. Cut five 5½-inch strips across the short end of the fabric. Each of these can then be cut into four 5½-inch patches.

You will have a fairly large piece of fabric left when you are done. This will be enough to make binding if you'd rather try that than the commercial binding.

Cutting the Remaining Fabric

By comparison, cutting the other two fabrics is easy. You will need eighty 5½ × 5½-inch squares from each. Cut away the selvage first, and then cut the fabric into 5½-inch strips. Slice the strips into squares. You should be able to cut seven squares from each strip and easily get twelve strips from the 2 yards.

If you bought regular fabric for the backing, it will need to be cut and pieced. After straightening the ends, cut the fabric in half the short way. In other words, you need to have two 3-yard lengths of the fabric. Cut the selvages away from both sides of both lengths. Split one of the lengths down the center the long way, creating two strips of fabric 3 yards by about 21 inches. If your fabric is less than 42 inches wide or if the selvages are unusually deep, you may need to trim an inch or so off the borders of the cover. That's easily done later.

Sew the two narrow strips on either side of the remaining length of fabric. This puts the seams near the edges of the bed instead of right down the center.

Piecing It All Together

Use your newly cut pieces to lay out a few 9-Patch blocks. Place some of the vertical panels between them to get an idea of what your quilt will look like. Decide if you want to make all the blocks alike or if you want the two coordinating fabrics to take turns being in the corner positions.

Sew the squares into rows and press the seams. Matching the seams as closely as possible, sew the rows into blocks. Press these seams as well.

Next, set aside the five blocks that will be along the right side of the quilt. If your blocks are all the same, it won't matter which five you set aside. With the rest of the blocks near your sewing machine, take one of the shorter horizontal panel strips. With it face-up, position one of the blocks face-down on top of it. Sew a ¼-inch seam. When you get to the end of the block, backstitch a few stitches. Position the next block on top of the panel at the end of the first block. The two blocks can touch but must not overlap. Sew off the first block and onto the second block about three stitches. Backstitch to the edge of the block and continue along the block.

Repeat with a third block on this panel piece and the rest of the blocks on the other two horizontal panel pieces. Cut the blocks apart carefully, keeping your cut straight on the panel. Sew the block-panel pieces and the right-side blocks together to form five rows of four blocks. Press the seams toward the panels.

Being careful not to stretch the panel fabric, sew one of the horizontal panels to one of the rows of blocks. Trim to the proper length. Sew all the rows of blocks together with the horizontal panels between them, and press all the seams toward the panels.

Sew border strips on either side of the quilt top and trim to the proper length. After these seams are pressed, sew the two end borders in place and press them as well.

Finishing Your First Quilt

Layer the quilt as described at the beginning of Chapter 7. Baste it all over with large safety pins. Decide on the placement of your ties. I'd suggest placing a tie in the middle of the center squares, in the middle of the vertical panels, and along the horizontal panels even with the other ties. Be sure to place some ties on the borders as well. Refer back to the beginning of Chapter 9 for specific instructions on tying and remove the basting pins as you tie.

Trim the edges of your quilt to make the layers even. Round off the corners, making sure that you cut them all the same.

Making a pattern from a large dinner plate will take some of the guesswork out of this step.

Sew the binding on as described at the beginning of Chapter 10.

Changing the Pattern

Most quilt patterns can be easily changed to accommodate different size beds. The 7-inch border can be decreased or increased to make minor changes. The size or number of blocks can be changed to make greater alterations. Adding one more block to each row of this pattern would make a king-size quilt. Be sure to buy extra fabric to accommodate longer end borders and horizontal panels as well as more of the smaller pieces. Making six of the blocks described and arranging them in three rows of two with the 3-inch panels between them and 2-inch borders would make a 37 × 55-inch baby quilt.

You can also use this pattern with scraps and fat quarters. You can get by with 2½ yards of fabric for the borders and panels if you don't use it for the center of the blocks. You can get either nine or twelve squares from a fat quarter, depending on the fabric's original width, which means you will need anywhere between fourteen and twenty fat quarters for the blocks.

The patches, of course, can be any size you want. Instead of using panels between the blocks you can alternate the 9-Patch blocks with plain blocks. Use your imagination, and have fun.

Five of Diamonds for Experienced Quilters

This is a more advanced version of the 9-Patch quilt. The 9-Patch blocks are set on point and boxed in by four large triangles made from the same fabric as four of the squares in the block. The effect is for the other five squares, diamonds now because they are on point, to stand out in this field of contrasting fabric. Pairing up the fabrics for the blocks is only part of the fun. A large appliqué adds a personal touch.

Fabrics

You can make the blocks any size you want, but 4-inch (finished size) squares will make 12-inch 9-Patches. The triangles that surround them will be 9½-inch (cut size) squares split diagonally. You can cut the four triangular corners and four of the squares out of one fat quarter. You can cut the five interior "diamonds" for two blocks from one fat quarter.

I made a double bed–size quilt by arranging six rows of four blocks. I added a 9-inch border to the sides and bottom but not to the top, because I wanted to see the row of blocks across the pillows. At the bottom corners, I placed matching 9-Patches. When the quilt is on the bed, these two blocks hang on point like the 9-Patches on the rest of the quilt.

To make a quilt this size, you will need about thirty-six fat quarters or equivalent scraps, plus fabric for the borders. As you pair up the fabrics for the blocks, make sure you have enough contrast in the intensity of the colors so the five "diamonds" show up. Try looking at your fabric pairs from a distance or in relatively low light to make sure they don't blend so well that the diamond pattern disappears.

Appliqué

Make some sketches of your appliqué design or use a picture if you can find one. Don't get too complicated unless you are experienced with appliqué. You can pick up a theme you've discovered in the fabrics you've chosen. Several of the fabrics that I used in my quilt have little dragonflies, and I used one as a guide to design a large dragonfly.

You might want to create a design that represents your occupation or hobby. A stack of books, a compass, a watering can, a chess piece, or nearly anything can be simplified and depicted in appliqué.

For my dragonfly, I wanted to be able to "see through" his wings, so I cut out the centers. Knowing this would make the fabric sort of flimsy, I traced my pattern on fusible interfacing, ironed it to the back of my fabric, and cut the pieces out ¼-inch beyond the interfacing. This stiffened the fabric enough to let me place it more smoothly, and it also gave me a guide for turning under the raw edges.

Construction

Sew your 9-Patches together and then add the triangle corners. Be careful not to stretch the bias edges of the triangles. Lay the blocks out to arrange them. While you're at it, determine where you'll want your appliqué. It's best if you have the pieces cut so you can see how they'll look against the blocks.

My dragonfly has very pale wings that match one of the border fabrics. I wanted to be sure he showed up, so I positioned two of my darkest blocks near the lower right-hand corner of the quilt where I wanted him to alight. His body is made from one of the background fabrics so I positioned the block with that fabric far away from the corner.

My dragonfly's larger pair of wings have a span of about 22 inches, so while he is primarily on one block, he extends into three others. I sewed these four blocks together and then placed and hand appliquéd my dragonfly. This kept me from having to struggle with an entire quilt top while I sewed.

Finish your quilt as usual. You can tie or machine or hand quilt, whichever you like.

Quilting Suggestion

Give some thought to quilting a design that complements your appliqué. I wanted to repeat the dragonfly shape in hand quilting several times on my quilt and then fill in between them with looping "flight paths" trailing my stitched dragonflies. I used my appliqué pattern to draw the same shape on three overlapped sheets of paper. I did a little work on the wings to make the shape more like a continuous-stitch quilting design. When I was satisfied, I made twelve photocopies of the pages and taped each of the dragonflies together. That way I could arrange and rearrange the dragonflies on my quilt top until they were spaced the way I wanted them. Using straight pins at the corners of my patterns to hold them in place, I slipped dressmaker's carbon under the patterns and traced the designs. I drew the flight paths between the dragonflies freehand, and it was ready to layer and quilt.

Index